Leaves from Daddy G.O's Table VOL. 3

Prosperity

A Collection of Messages on Prosperity by E. A. Adeboye | Also Included: Over 150 Prayers for Financial Breakthrough

E. A. ADEBOYE

Copyright © 2017 Enoch Adeboye

All Rights Reserved: No Portion of this book may be used without the written permission of the Author, with the exception of brief excerpts in magazines, articles, reviews, group and Church teachings. All Bible quotations are taken from the King James Version of the Bible.

Published & Printed by: Printme Communication Company

40, Sanusi Street, Somolu, Lagos, Nigeria, Tel: +234-8098686936, 8023686936

Email: pmcc03@yahoo.com

Under a special arrangement with SPANNERS PUBLISHING LIMITED

For testimonies and comments:

E-mail: spannerspublishingltd@gmail.com

Tel:+2347063771166, +2348033048245, +353899646326, +353857505353

Contents

PROLOGUE _____ 5
INTRODUCTION _____ 9
PREFACE _____ 12
DEDICATION _____ 14
ACKNOWLEDGMENTS _____ 15
CHAPTER 1: FROM ZERO TO UNLIMITED WEALTH _ 18
CHAPTER 2: THE WONDERS OF EXPLOITS _____ 25
CHAPTER 3: THE WONDERS OF HIS FAVOR _____ 39
CHAPTER 4: GOD WILL MAKE YOU LAUGH _____ 55
CHAPTER 5: THE INSTRUCTOR _____ 66
CHAPTER 6: SECRETS OF ABUNDANCE _____ 79
CHAPTER 7: UNLIMITED FINANCIAL BREAKTHROUGH _____ 89
CHAPTER 8: GREAT EXPECTATION _____ 103
CHAPTER 9: THE KEYS OF DAVID _____ 114
CHAPTER 10: THE SECRETS OF GREAT SEEDS _____ 123
CHAPTER 11: MADE GREAT BY GRACE _____ 137
CHAPTER 12: YOUR PROSPERITY IS SETTLED _____ 152
CHAPTER 13: DELIVERANCE FROM POVERTY _____ 162
CHAPTER 14: HELP IS ON THE WAY _____ 180
CHAPTER 15: THE BLESSED OF THE LORD _____ 190
CHAPTER 16: OVERFLOWING GREATNESS _____ 203
CHAPTER 17: RIVERS OF LIVING WATERS _____ 210
CHAPTER 18: PEACE LIKE A RIVER _____ 225

CHAPTER 19: THE SECRETS OF OVERFLOW _____ 239
CHAPTER 20: THE SUREST WAY TO PROSPERITY _ 251
CHAPTER 21: THE LAWS OF HARVEST _____ 262
CHAPTER 22: REJECTING RICHES _____ 271
CHAPTER 23: THE WONDERS OF HIS NAME_____ 284
CHAPTER 24: THE WONDERS OF HIS PRAISE _____ 298
CHAPTER 25: SOUNDS FROM HEAVEN_____308
BIBLIOGRAPHY_____ 316
ABOUT THE EDITOR _____ 321

PROLOGUE

The word 'prosperity' is interpreted differently by different people. Likewise, its degree of acceptance even among Christians varies. To those in the secular world prosperity may mean all sorts of things. Whereas some Christians think it is a good thing, some others accept it with a pinch of salt. This is so because they think as Christians we should only be preoccupied by the coming of our Lord Jesus Christ, while we leave other aspects of life untouched. Another school of thought believes that prosperity referred to in the scriptures has to do with heaven alone – we will only prosper when we get to heaven.

When some Christians see those who are prospering materially, they conclude that they have backslid. This is unbiblical and a lie from the devil himself. Have you ever thought about it that to spread the Gospel of our Lord Jesus Christ, we need lots of money? To let everyone know that Jesus is coming soon, we need huge budgets to make it happen. Why do you think the devil has continued to discourage Christians about

God's will for them that they prosper? It is so he can limit the spread of the Gospel through its various ministries. Is that not why secular stations will never allow you broadcast your church programs on air unless you can afford their airtime?

God expects us to be blessings to the world. We are called to be the salt of the earth. How can one be a blessing when his life is chained in the shackles of poverty? What evidence will you then have to tell someone that God is good? To cater for the less privileged and destitute, you cannot be a destitute yourself. Do not allow anyone to deceive you into believing that wealth is only for the worldly. In fact, the Almighty God has promised that the wealth of the wicked will be transferred to the righteous ones in our time (Proverbs 13:22).

However, the children of the world have their way of getting wealth from their father, the devil. As children of God on the other hand, we cannot go the same way with the world. God has His way of prospering His children. All we need to do is to be patient and key into His divine principles which are sure. Some claim to be Christians, but fail to apply God's principles of exceeding wealth. They try to do it like the world. Worldly principles will never work in the Kingdom of God. This explains the reason why so many Christians are still struggling with poverty. Other reasons may include some demonic interference or blockage. But with the power of God, it is broken in the name of Jesus, if you apply the right principles. These principles are explained in details in this volume.

How you get wealth matters to God. Wealth gotten by unfair means surely brings lots of sorrow with it. Only the Almighty God gives wealth that comes with peace beyond human understanding. Do not be in a hurry to accept fake wealth from satan. Exceeding greatness is certain with God, if you are diligent and faithful.

These among many other reasons are why this volume has carefully looked into various dimensions of prosperity that we are supposed to enjoy as children of God. What is God's mind about prosperity? What are the principles of exceeding prosperity? Why do you need to prosper? What should you do with your prosperity? How can you prosper?. As you read this volume and say the prayers in each of the twenty five chapters, I pray that the God of prosperity will locate you and single you out for blessings in Jesus' name.

However, prosperity will be meaningless if you have not given your life to Christ, because the blessings of the Lord makes rich and adds no sorrow with it (Proverbs10:22). You may also want to rededicate your life and have a brand new beginning with Him in order to be sure of your salvation.

As you desire to embark on the journey of exceeding greatness, please say the following prayer of salvation:

Lord Jesus, I come to You as I am. I acknowledge that I am a sinner. I repent of all my sins. I come to You with humility of heart asking for Your mercy and forgiveness. I believe Jesus Christ died on the cross of Calvary for my sins. Jesus save me. Holy Spirit come into my heart as from today and direct me in all my ways. Thank you Father for saving me in Jesus name, Amen.

If you have said the above prayers, congratulations. Your exceeding greatness is sure!

Pastor E.A. Adeboye

INTRODUCTION

I feel highly honoured, privileged and humbled to have been called upon by the facilitator/editor of these glorious books, Pastor Taiwo Olukoyede, to serve as the General Editor/Chairman Editorial Board.

The books, dedicated to the glory of God upon the life and ministry of our Father in the Lord, the General Overseer of the Redeemed Christian Church Of God, Worldwide, Pastor E.A Adeboye, as he turns 75 years of age, consist of 75 prayerfully selected sermons/teachings of Pastor E.A Adeboye published in volumes, namely: Holiness, Healing and Prosperity under the title "Leaves From Daddy GO's Table". The title was derived from the book of Revelation Chapter 22 verses 1 and 2:

"And he shewed me a pure river of water of life, clear as crystal, proceeding out of the throne of God and of the Lamb. In the midst of the street of it, and on either side of the river, was there the tree of life, which bare twelve

manner of fruits, and yielded her fruit every month: and the leaves of the tree were for the healing of the nations."

The concept was brought about in the course of my meeting with Pastor Olukoyede in my office in the year 2015, in pursuant of Daddy GO's vision on Church Planting and Evangelism, and a follow up to what the Holy Spirit revealed to me in the year 2014, when I visited Ireland as a Guest Minister during the 5th year anniversary of *RCCG* Joseph's Palace, Dublin, on the invitation of Pastor Nathan Lesado, under the leadership of Pastor Tunde Adebayo-Oke (Regional Pastor, RCCG, Republic of Ireland).

As the General Overseer of th*Reedeemed Christian Church of G,od* Worldwide, our Father in the Lord, Pastor E. A Adeboye, popularly referred to as "Daddy GO" by all his children all over the world, has worked tirelessly with the help of the Holy Spirit to expand the Church's outreach, home and abroad. One of the well-known programmes of the Church is the Holy Ghost Service, an all-night miracle service that holds on the first Friday of every month at the Redemption Camp, Km. 46, Lagos-Ibadan Express Way, Nigeria.

The Holy Ghost Service now holds in different parts of the world, which includes Ireland, The United Kingdom, India, USA, Canada, South-Africa, Australia, Dubai, Ghana, the Philipines and many more. Today, the Church, which was practically unknown when he took over the mandate of leadership, now has parishes in almost 192 countries, including more than 37,000 in Nigeria.

His life is an embodiment of holiness enveloped in absolute separation and total devotion unto God, which is the major focus of his teachings/sermons as echoed in these Volumes.

I have read the books over and over again with each reading bringing about a new depth of spiritual knowledge and understanding. As you study each Volume, please take time to say the prayers in each chapter with great expectation. The Almighty God will perfect everything concerning you, and make you exceedingly great, in the mighty name of Jesus.

Pastor Joseph Adeyokunnu

RCCG Headquarters, Redemption Camp,

Nigeria.

PREFACE

Leaves from Daddy GO's Table is a collection of 75 prayerfully selected sermons of Pastor E. A. Adeboye over the years, which runs in three volumes: **Holiness**, **Healing** and **Prosperity**.

The title was revealed to me in the course of the RCCG 50 days prayer and fasting exercise for 2016, declared by our father in the Lord, Pastor E. A. Adeboye.

Towards the end of the prayer and fasting period, I was led by the Spirit of God to the Book of Revelation Chapter 22 verses 1&2:

"1 And he shewed me a pure river of water of life, clear as crystal, proceeding out of the throne of God and of the Lamb.

2 In the midst of the street of it, and on either side of the river, was there the tree of life, which bare twelve manner of fruits, and yielded her fruit every month: and the leaves of the tree were for the healing of the nations."

The idea to publish the books was originally conceived by me through the manifestation of the Holy Spirit during one of my meetings with my spiritual father, Pastor Joseph Adeyokunnu, in his office at the RCCG Headquarters in 2015, as a follow-up to his prophecy in 2014 of my deeper involvement in ministerial work from the background of Legal Practice.

Through several teachings of Pastor E.A Adeboye, the books written in a user-friendly style with copious quotes of relevant scriptures, identify Holiness as the core foundation for healing, financial and spiritual empowerment, and most importantly, as a sure passport for Heaven-bound Christians.

By the grace of God, the books shall bring healing, peace and joy to individuals, families, institutions, and nations of the world, and further serve as indispensable memoirs to future generations, as well as essential tools of personal salvation, soul winning and empowerment.

Taiwo Olukoyede

RCCG Joseph's Palace

Dublin, Ireland.

DEDICATION

To the glory of God upon the life of our Mummy in Israel Pastor [Mrs.] Folu Adeboye for her relentless service to the Mission in the areas of Prayers, Welfare and Evangelism.

ACKNOWLEDGMENTS

Glory be to God Almighty, who has given our Father in the Lord, Pastor E.A. Adeboye, as a gift to our present generation, whose Church planting vision created an open and welcoming platform for the conception and successful execution of this project. I thank my spiritual mentor, Pastor Joseph Adeyokunnu, for embracing the idea of this book when it was first mentioned to him, and for his ingenuity in devising a method that enabled the production of the book.

I thank Pastor Julius Olalekan, who bought into Dadd'y GO s church planting vision by sending forth a transformational leader, Pastor Lesado Nathan, towards the planting of Joseph's Palace, Dublin. The exercise would have been futile without the co-operation of our amiable Pastor Tunde Adebayo-Oke (Regional Pastor, RCCG, Ireland), who created a conducive environment for the take-off of Joseph's Palace, Dublin, with supportive, loving and God-fearing ministers and workers led by Pastor Deji Coo, the Regional Administrator.

I thank the members and workers of RCCG Lagos Province 29, for giving me the opportunity to serve at various capacities, and our Provincial Pastor, Pastor Kolawole Ayinla, for his generosity and spiritual wisdom, having to cope with my absences in the course of my stay in Ireland.

My wife, Olufemi Olukoyede, has performed wonderfully well as a valuable and inestimable editorial assistant, coupled with the support and co-operation of our children even at odd hours. I also thank our contributing editors, Dr. (Mrs.) Olusola Olatunbosun, Pastor (Mrs.) Ronke Nathan, Pastor Ifeoluwa Akindayomi and Barr. Goddy Enaiho, for their time and support. My appreciation goes to Pastor Tony Olukoyede, Pastors Segun & Yoana Philips, Pastor Ola Olukoyede, Mr. & Mrs. Remi Balogun, Sis. Oluwatosin Idowu, Evang. Segun Dabiri, Pastor Ayodele Oladeji and Deji West, for expending their invaluable resources towards the success of this project.

I must also place on record the exemplary leadership/mentorship motivational roles of ourhefarst in the ministry, Pastor Joseph Obayemi and Pastor JohnsoOndesola in their respective areas of calling.

Finally, I thank our publishers, Printme Communication Company, led by its Managing Director, Brother Justice kAul,o its Editing Director, Victor Akarachi Nwogu, andet hentire staff of the company for their careful attention to delt aait every stage of the production of this book.

For the conception and successful completion of this glorious work, Glory be to God Almighty!

Taiwo Olukoyede

CHAPTER 1: FROM ZERO TO UNLIMITED WEALTH

Now there cried a certain woman of the wives of the sons of the prophets unto Elisha, saying, Thy servant my husband is dead; and thou knowest that thy servant did fear the LORD: and the creditor is come to take unto him my two sons to be bondmen. And Elisha said unto her, What shall I do for thee? tell me, what hast thou in the house? And she said, Thine handmaid hath not anything in the house, save a pot of oil. Then he said, Go, borrow thee vessels abroad of all thy neighbours, even empty vessels; borrow not a few. And when thou art come in, thou shalt shut the door upon thee and upon thy sons, and shalt pour out into all those vessels, and thou shalt set aside that which is full. So she went from him, and shut the door upon her and upon her sons, who brought the vessels to her; and she poured out. And it came to pass, when the vessels were full, that she said unto her son, Bring me yet a vessel. And he said unto her, There is not a vessel more. And the oil stayed. Then she came and told the man of God. And he said, Go, sell the oil, and pay thy debt, and live thou and thy children of the rest. And it fell on a day, that Elisha passed to Shunem, where was a great woman; and she constrained him to eat bread. And so it was, that as oft as he passed by, he turned in thither to eat bread. 2 Kings 4:1-8.

The scriptures have given us easy principles to follow on what it takes to attain the ultimate financial breakthrough. The hobbies of the Almighty God are doing signs and wonders. Whenever a need arises, Jehovah Jireh presents Himself at the scene to meet it. Your needs provide God with the opportunity to demonstrate His power and greatness. God is constantly searching for embarrassing situations to demonstrate His power and uncommon ability, and to turn hopeless financial situations around.

The interesting thing about our God is that He does not need to struggle in order to make you wealthy. He can turn a pauper into a billionaire overnight. He is in the job of taking people from the lowest positions in life and planting their feet on the highest pinnacle of unlimited wealth.

The presence of God in any situation turns such situations around from negative into positive. When God comes into circumstances, a debtor would become a lender to nations; a widow would become the richest person in the community; those whose survival depends on the rich would begin to lend to the rich. A man who is under heavy bondage of debt can be transformed by God to one who lends to financial institutions. It only takes an encounter with God.

This chapter began with a beautiful story from the Bible, which illustrates the fact that the poorest can become the richest, and an outcast can become a celebrity. When you have an encounter with God and carry out instructions, your story will become a reference point for the world for good. A widow who had lost every hope had an encounter with God through Elisha, the prophet. The miracle she received altered the course of her life forever.

In order to be catapulted from a zero financial condition to unlimited wealth, there are some lessons we should learn from this widow.

She Desperately Cried for Help

We see from the passage that the journey to the realm of unlimited financial breakthroughs starts with a desperate cry unto God. God is always willing to interfere in our affairs when we cry unto Him for help.

And ye shall seek me, and find me, when ye shall search for me with all your heart. Jeremiah 29:13

If you are content with where you are, your prayer will be far from being desperate. But when you are really tired of your condition, you will cry out to God in desperation (Adeboye, 2005). The text above did not record that the widow just had a chat with Elisha. She rather cried unto him because she was in desperate need of a miracle. Also, the widow did not murmur before Elisha, but she cried. She also did not grumble to attract the attention of the prophet. She cried out for divine intervention.

God Answers through His Servants

Each time you cry unto God, He grants your request. When the woman cried to the man of God, he asked her, "What can I do for you?" This demonstrates God's willingness to answer prayers.

Offer unto God thanksgiving; and pay thy vows unto the most High: And call upon me in the day of trouble: I will deliver thee, and thou shalt glorify me Psalm 50:13-14

God makes it no secret that if you cry unto Him, He will answer you. God does not ignore desperate cries from pure hearts. The man of God asked the widow what she wanted, she made her requests known, and God met her at the point of her need. Such will be your portion in Jesus' name.

God Directed Her

The man of God gave her certain specific instructions. She was told to borrow empty vessels from her neighbours and fill all the vessels with the oil. Your journey to unlimited wealth will begin today, and God will give you step by step guidelines in Jesus' name.

Whenever God wants to give someone a major breakthrough, He guides the person. Therefore, you must pay attention when God speaks, listening carefully to His instructions. Peter and his colleagues toiled all night and caught no fish. However, when Jesus gave him specific instruction to cast his net into the deep for a catch, he obeyed (Luke 5:1-7). If Peter failed to obey divine instructions he would have missed the miracle.

If you are willing to obey God, He will guide you step by step; one at a time, until you reach the apex of your financial breakthrough (Adeboye, 2005).

God Blessed Her in Her Neighborhood

The woman was living in a predominantly poor neighbourhood. A closer study of the story suggests that most of her neighbours were poor. This explains why they had lots of empty vessels to spare. What God intends to do for you is that in the midst of the same neighbours you have, you will find your greatest opportunity.

You might not have noticed that you may be living in the midst of opportunities. Where you live right now, there are countless miracles. God will inspire you to discover your miracles around you in Jesus' name.

There was famine in the land where Isaac was, and he wanted to move out of his neighbourhood. But God specifically instructed him to stay where he was and sow there. He obeyed God, and God prospered him in that land ravaged with famine (Genesis 26:1-14).

In the same vein, God is going to prosper you no matter the economic situation in your country.

Prayer Points

1. Oh Lord, cause me to see opportunities for my financial breakthrough, in the name of Jesus.

2. My Father, I cry unto you: Change my condition, i'n Jesus name!

3. Eternal Rock of Ages, wipe out the trace of poverty in my lineage, in Jesus' name.

4. Almighty God, position me in my place of unlimited prosperity in Jesus' name.

5. Daddy, you are my Source; I receive my financial breakthrough now, in Jesus' name.

CHAPTER 2: THE WONDERS OF EXPLOITS

And king Solomon offered a sacrifice of twenty and two thousand oxen, and an hundred and twenty thousand sheep: so the king and all the people dedicated the house of God. – 2 Chronicles 7:5

To begin this chapter, I just want to ask you a simple question: What exploits will you do if God prospers you? What is your reason for asking God to prosper you? Do you want to prosper to marry seven wives, build a hundred houses, and buy two hundred cars?

Abraham was told by the Almighty God that he was going to be blessed. In Genesis 12:7-8, based on the promise, Abraham built an altar and worshiped God.

And the LORD appeared unto Abram, and said, Unto thy seed will I give this land: and

there builded he an altar unto the LORD, who appeared unto him. And he removed from thence unto a mountain on the east of Bethel, and pitched his tent, having Bethel on the west, and Hai on the east: and there he builded an altar unto the LORD, and called upon the name of the LORD. – Genesis 12:7-8

Abraham demonstrated his devotion to God by building an altar to worship God based on just promises. By the time we get to Genesis 13:1-4, when the blessings started coming, Abraham went straight to the altar and worshiped God again.

And Abram went up out of Egypt, he, and his wife, and all that he had, and Lot with him, into the south. And Abram was very rich in cattle, in silver, and in gold. And he went on his journeys from the south even to Bethel, unto the place where his tent had been at the beginning, between Bethel and Hai; Unto the place of the altar, which he had made there at the first: and there Abram called on the name of the LORD. – Genesis 13:1-4

Proceeding to Genesis 22:1-18, Abraham had become really blessed. He also demonstrated to God that he loved Him more than every other thing, including his very precious son, Isaac.

And it came to pass after these things, that God did tempt Abraham, and said unto him, Abraham: and he said, Behold, here I am. And he said, Take now thy son, thine only son Isaac, whom thou lovest, and get thee into the land of Moriah; and offer him there for a burnt offering upon one of the mountains which I will tell thee of. And Abraham rose up early in the morning, and saddled his ass, and took two of his young men with him, and Isaac his son, and clave the wood for the burnt offering, and rose up, and went unto the place of which God had told him. Then on the third day Abraham lifted up his eyes, and saw the place afar off. And Abraham said unto his young men, Abide ye here with the ass; and I and the lad will go yonder and worship, and come again to you. And Abraham took the wood of the burnt offering, and laid it upon Isaac his son; and he took the fire in his hand, and a knife; and they went both of them together. And Isaac spake unto

Abraham his father, and said, My father: and he said, Here am I, my son. And he said, Behold the fire and the wood: but where is the lamb for a burnt offering? And Abraham said, My son, God will provide himself a lamb for a burnt offering: so they went both of them together. And they came to the place which God had told him of; and Abraham built an altar there, and laid the wood in order, and bound Isaac his son, and laid him on the altar upon the wood. And Abraham stretched forth his hand, and took the knife to slay his son. And the angel of the LORD called unto him out of heaven, and said, Abraham, Abraham: and he said, Heream I. And he said, Lay not thine hand upon the lad, neither do thou any thing unto him: for now I know that thou fearest God, seeing thou hast not withheld thy son, thine only son from me. And Abraham lifted up his eyes, and looked, and behold behind him a ram caught in a thicket by his horns: and Abraham went and took the ram, and offered him up for a burnt offering in the stead of his son. And Abraham called the name of that place Jehovahjireh: as it is said to this day, In the mount of the LORD it shall be seen. And the angel of the LORD called unto Abraham out of heaven the second time, And said, By myself have I sworn, saith the LORD, for because thou hast done this thing, and hast not withheld thy son, thine only son: That in blessing I will bless thee, and in multiplying I will multiply thy seed as the stars of the heaven, and as the sand which is upon the sea shore; and thy seed shall possess the gate of his enemies; And in thy seed shall all the nations of the earth be blessed; because thou hast obeyed my voice. – Genesis 22:1-18

When we get to Genesis 24:34-35, we are not surprised that the testimony of Abraham's servant is that God has prospered his master greatly.

And he said, I am Abraham's servant. And the LORD hath blessed my master greatly; and he is become great: and he hath given him flocks, and herds, and silver, and gold, and menservants, and maidservants, and camels, and asses. – Genesis 24:34-35

What will you do if God Prospers you?

David is a great example. The Almighty God picked him from nowhere and gave him a breakthrough. What did he do with the prosperity? He said he wanted to build a temple for God. God refused because his hands were stained with blood. In spite of God's rejection of his offer, he did something spectacular. He donated all the materials that would be needed to build the temple. Whoever was going to build the temple would not have to spend anything of his own if he wishes. David made sufficient provision available before he died. The Bible records that everything Solomon needed to build God's temple was provided by David.

Now, behold, in my trouble I have prepared for the house of the LORD an hundred thousand talents of gold, and a thousand thousand talents of silver; and of brass and iron without weight; for it is in abundance: timber also and stone have I prepared; and thou mayest add thereto. Moreover there are workmen with thee in abundance, hewers and workers of stone and timber, and all manner of cunning men for every manner of work. Of the gold, the silver, and the brass, and the iron, there is no number. Arise therefore, and be doing, and the LORD be with thee. — 1 Chronicles 22:14-16

In 2 Samuel 24:22-24, we discover that David never gave God an offering that did not cost him something. He never gave a casual offering. Every time David had an opportunity to give to God, he gave until he felt like he had given something.

And Araunah said unto David, Let my lord the king take and offer up what seemeth good unto him: behold, here be oxen for burnt sacrifice, and threshing instruments and other instruments of the oxen for wood. All these things did Araunah, as a king, give unto the king. And Araunah said unto the king, The LORD thy God accept thee. And the king said unto Araunah, Nay; but I will surely buy it of thee at a price: neither will I offer burnt offerings unto the LORD my God of that which doth cost me nothing. So David bought the threshingfloor and the oxen for fifty shekels of silver . – 2 Samuel 24:22-24

Solomon, David's son, followed in the footsteps of his father. In 2 Chronicles 1, Solomon had his first opportunity to give offering to God. He gave one thousand bullocks.

And Solomon went up thither to the brasen altar before the LORD, which was at the tabernacle of the congregation, and offered a thousand burnt offerings upon it. In that night did God appear unto Solomon, and said unto him, Ask what I shall give thee. And Solomon said unto God, Thou hast shewed great mercy unto David my father, and hast made me to reign in his stead. Now, O LORD God, let thy promise unto David my father be established: for thou hast made me king over a people like the dust of the earth in multitude. Give me now wisdom and knowledge, that I may go out and come in before this people: for who can judge this thy people, that is so great? And God said to Solomon, Because this was in thine heart, and thou hast not asked riches, wealth, or honour, nor the life of thine enemies, neither yet hast asked long life; but hast asked wisdom and knowledge for thyself, that thou mayest judge my people, over whom I have made thee king: Wisdom and knowledge is granted unto thee; and I will give thee riches, and wealth, and honour, such as none of the kings have had that have been before thee, neither shall there any after thee have the like. – 2 Chronicles 1:6-12

Everyone, including God, was amazed at Solomon's offering. No one had seen such an offering before. God blessed him beyond description as a result. However, Solomon was not done. The next time he gave an offering, he moved to twenty two thousand oxen! That was not all. He also offered with it a hundred and twenty thousand sheep!

And king Solomon offered a sacrifice of twenty and two thousand oxen, and an hundred and twenty thousand sheep: so the king and all the people dedicated the house of God. – 2 Chronicles 7:5

Solomon shows us what it means for God to prosper a righteous man.

What about the Shunammite woman? When God prospered her, how did she spend the money? She started by feeding the man of God, and then built the prophet a house. What will you do if God prospers you?

And it fell on a day, that Elisha passed to Shunem, where was a great woman; and she constrained him to eat bread. And so it was, that as oft as he passed by, he turned in

thither to eat bread. And she said unto her husband, Behold now, I perceive that this isan holy man of God, which passeth by us continually. Let us make a little chamber, I pray thee, on the wall; and let us set for him there a bed, and a table, and a stool, and a candlestick: and it shall be, when he cometh to us, that he shall turn in thither. And it fell on a day, that he came thither, and he turned into the chamber, and lay there. And he said to Gehazi his servant, Call this Shunammite. And when he had called her, she stood before him. And he said unto him, Say now unto her, Behold, thou hast been careful for us with all this care; what is to be done for thee? wouldest thou be spoken for to the king, or to the captain of the host? And she answered, I dwell among mine own people. And he said, What then is to be done for her? And Gehazi answered, Verily she hath no child, and her husband is old. And he said, Call her. And when he had called her, she stood in the door. And he said, About this season, according to the time of life, thou shalt embrace a son. And she said, Nay, my lord, thou man of God, do not lie unto thine handmaid. And the woman conceived, and bare a son at that season that Elisha had said unto her, according to the time of life. – 2 Kings 4:8-17

When we read the story of the widow's mite, what is the implication?

And Jesus sat over against the treasury, and beheld how the people cast money into the treasury: and many that were rich cast in much. And there came a certain poor widow, and she threw in two mites, which make a farthing. And he called unto him his disciples, and saith unto them, Verily I say unto you, That this poor widow hath cast more in, than all they which have cast into the treasury: For all they did cast in of their abundance; but she of her want did cast in all that she had, even all her living. – Mark 12:41-44

What is the significance in what she did? Jesus Christ commended her because she gave everything she had.

She was saying to God:" I don't have much, but this is all I have. You can have it all!"

God is not just looking at your prayers; He is looking also at your motive. The Bible says that actions are weighed by God.

Talk no more so exceeding proudly; let not arrogancy come out of your mouth: for the LORD is a God of knowledge, and by him actions are weighed. – 1 Samuel 2:3

You may be praying; "God make me the richest man on earth"; " O Lord, prosper me; make me rich". The Lord is saying, "Alright. If I give you the wealth, what will you do with it?"

There was a young man who came to me a long time ago, and asked me to pray for him. He said he wanted to be among one of the three people that will be sponsoring our convention. He was just a salary earner. I prayed for him, the following week, he was sacked from his place of work. He was sad and came to me. I asked him if he thought he could sponsor the convention from his salary. God simply closed that door so that he could open unto him an effectual door of wealth. The following convention, he came and gave me ten million naira equivalent of today's currency rate. God took him to the top.

Another young man came to me and asked me to pray for him. He said he was tired of poverty and was ready to do God's will if he prospers him. We prayed together and after two weeks, he got a great contract. I stopped seeing him for a while. After some time again I met him and he said I should still pray for him to get another contract. I asked hi"mW, hat happened to the other contract?" He replied,"It went well. Glory be to Go" dT! hen I queried, "I thought you said you were ready to do God's wil"l? H e responded, "That was just the first contract; God should understand. Pray for me to get another one." Sadly, that was the end of his prosperity.

The question comes to you again: If God prospers you, what exploits will you do for Him?

Action:

Get a piece of paper and write down what you will do for God if He prospers you.

Prayer Points

1. Lord, before you is my vow when you prosper me. Grant me the will to fulfil it, in the name of Jesus.

2. Father, let every dream of exploits I have for you come to pass, in the name of Jesus.

3. Father, use me as your instrument of financial blessing to generations, in the name of Jesus.

4. Father, remove greed from my life, in the name of Jesus.

5. Father, cure me of every fleshly lust that is hindering me from receiving your financial release, in the name of Jesus.

CHAPTER 3: THE WONDERS OF HIS FAVOR

I returned, and saw under the sun, that the race is not to the swift, nor the battle to the strong, neither yet bread to the wise, nor yet riches to men of understanding, nor yet favour to men of skill; but time and chance happeneth to them all. – Ecc. 9:11

Ponder on These Questions:

§   Why do I need divine favour in order to prosper?

§   Why do I need divine favour to succeed?

The answer lies in the above text. It is not how fast you are that will determine whether you will reach the goal or not. It is not how hard you work that will determine how successful you will become. In fact, the passage declares that it is not even how wise you are that will determine if you will get to the top or not. But God is the All in all. He is the Controller of everything.

The Bible says that our God is in the heavens, and He does as He pleases (Psalm 115:3). He does as he pleases and no one can query Him. He says He will be merciful on whomever he pleases, and have compassion on whosoever he wishes to.

For he saith to Moses, I will have mercy on whom I will have mercy, and I will have compassion on whom I will have compassion. – Romans 9:15

It is impossible for a vessel to query the porter. Who can look at the Lord and query his wisdom? Can the finger look at God and question Him saying, "Why did you make me so tiny?"

Woe unto him that striveth with his Maker! Let the potsherd strive with the potsherds of the earth. Shall the clay say to him that fashioneth it, What makest thou? or thy work, He hath no hands? – Isaiah 45:9

It is God who decides who will prosper. I pronounce into your life that you will find favour with God.

When I was at the University of Nigeria, Nsukka, I was a sportsman. There was a girl who was the fastest in the university. We went for a competition among other universities. We were so sure she would win a gold medal. No one could compete with her; she ran like the wind. She got to the finals and the race was about to kick off. On your marks, set, go! She took off and left her competitors meters behind. But when she had run about 10 meters, she suddenly fell. She got up and fell again. This happened trice.

The fourth time she fell, she began to crawl because she could not get up. That was how she lost the race. If you win a race, it is because God wants you to win. I pray for you that as you read this book, my Father in heaven will favour you, in the name of Jesus.

Diligence – is important. It pays off between God and man.

Seest thou a man diligent in his business? he shall stand before kings; he shall not stand before mean men. – Proverbs 22:29

God rewards those who are diligent in seeking him.

But without faith it is impossible to please him: for he that cometh to God must believe that he is, and that he is a rewarder of them that diligently seek him. – Hebrews 11:6

Diligence is great; but it is not enough. Yoruba elders have a saying that it does not matter how hard you struggle unless God favours you.

Sowing – As a son of a farmer, I saw my father plant yam seedlings into the soil when the first rain of the year falls. He planted the best seeds always. My father did not sow any seed that was not absolutely good. We always wondered why he kept planting the best seeds. The reason is because whatever you plant in a year determines what you harvest the next year. Galatians 6:7 makes it very clear:

"Be not deceived; God is not mocked: for whatsoever a man soweth, that shall he also reap."

The truth is that if you do not sow, you will not reap. If you sow sparingly, you will also reap sparingly.

But this I say, He which soweth sparingly shall reap also sparingly; and he which soweth bountifully shall reap also bountifully. – 2 Corinthians 9:6

Sowing is important; but it is not also enough.

I have planted, Apollos watered; but God gave the increase. So then neither is he that planteth any thing, neither he that watereth; but God that giveth the increase. – 1 Corinthians 3:6-7

All that God has to do for you to fail is to remain neutral. He does not have to fight you for you to fail. He may not stop you from sowing and watering. But if He refuses to give the increase, failure is assured. I pray that God will never leave you alone. Diligence is important; sowing is important. But unless God blesses– gives the increase – efforts will be in vain. Proverbs 10:22 makes it clear:

The blessing of the LORD, it maketh rich, and he addeth no sorrow with it.

Deuteronomy 8:11-18 also throws more light:

Beware that thou forget not the LORD thy God, in not keeping his commandments, and his judgments, and his statutes, which I command thee this day: Lest when thou hast eaten and art full, and hast built goodly houses, and dwelt therein; And when thy herds and thy flocks multiply, and thy silver and thy gold is multiplied, and all that thou hast is multiplied; Then thine heart be lifted up, and thou forget the LORD thy God, which brought thee forth out of the land of Egypt, from the house of bondage; Who led thee through that great and terrible wilderness, wherein were fiery serpents, and scorpions, and drought, where there was no water; who brought thee forth water out of the rock of flint; Who fed thee in the wilderness with manna, which thy fathers knew not, that he might humble thee, and that he might prove thee, to do thee good at thy latter end; And thou say in thine heart, My power and the might of mine hand hath gotten me this wealth. But thou shalt remember the LORD thy God: for it is he that giveth thee power to

get wealth, that he may establish his covenant which he sware unto thy fathers, as it is this day.

If you succeed, do not be proud. If you prosper, do not say it is because you know how to do it. It is God who gives the power to get wealth (Deuteronomy 8:18). It is God and God alone. In fact, there is nothing you are doing that others have not done before. There is nothing that you are doing that others are not even doing better. But God decides who to favour, and once He blesses you, you remain blessed.

Behold, I have received commandment to bless: and he hath blessed; and I cannot reverse it. – Numbers 23:20

When God blesses you, all the enemies in the world cannot stop that blessing. When God decides to favour you, He will do it in such a way that everybody begins to complain. In fact, you are not yet thoroughly blessed until everyone begins to criticise you. The Bible says that when Isaac sowed in the time of famine, God prospered him so much that the Philistines envied him. Imagine a whole nation envying a person! I pray for you that God will bless you so much that newspapers, TV stations, and all forms of media will begin to criticise you.

When God decides to favour you, He sets you up for a blessing. For example, in Luke 4:24-26, the story of the widow of Sarepta becomes compelling:

And he said, Verily I say unto you, No prophet is accepted in his own country. But I tell you of a truth, many widows were in Israel in the days of Elias, when the heaven was shut up three years and six months, when great famine was throughout all the land; But unto none of them was Elias sent, save unto Sarepta, a city of Sidon, unto a woman that was a widow.

Many widows in Israel needed a miracle, but God chose this particular widow. In 1 Kings 17:8-16, when Elijah came to her, she complained that she only had one last meal:

And the word of the LORD came unto him, saying, Arise, get thee to Zarephath, which belongeth to Zidon, and dwell there: behold, I have commanded a widow woman there to sustain thee. So he arose and went to

Zarephath. And when he came to the gate of the city, behold, the widow woman was there gathering of sticks: and he called to her, and said, Fetch me, I pray thee, a little water in a vessel, that I may drink. And as she was going to fetch it, he called to her, and said, Bring me, I pray thee, a morsel of bread in thine hand. And she said, As the LORD thy God liveth, I have not a cake, but an handful of meal in a barrel, and a little oil in a cruse: and, behold, I am gathering two sticks, that I may go in and dress it for me and my son, that we may eat it, and die. And Elijah said unto her, Fear not; go and do as thou hast said: but make me thereof a little cake first, and bring it unto me, and after make for thee and for thy son. For thus saith the LORD God of Israel, The barrel of meal shall not waste, neither shall the cruse of oil fail, until the day that the LORD sendeth rain upon the earth. And she went and did according to the saying of Elijah: and she, and he, and her house, did eat many days. And the barrel of meal wasted not, neither did the cruse of oil fail, according

to the word of the LORD, which he spake by Elijah. And it came to pass after these things, that the son of the woman, the mistress of the house, fell sick; and his sickness was so sore, that there was no breath left in him.

The prophet asked her to give him that last portion to eat. She obeyed, and the rest is history. Put yourself in her position of abundance then. Can you imagine everyone around her looking hungry, weak, haggard, and malnourished? But she was shining. Her only son was 'bubbling'. She had abundance. On the other hand, people would have gossiped and nosed around sayin"gW, e know your secret. It is because there is a prophet in your hous"e.So will people say when God has blessed you so much: " We know why you are prospering; it is because you are serving a Living God!"

God set up this widow for an unprecedented miracle. God requested for her last meal. Meaning, "Put me first, and let me see." God did this so that when other widows complain to Him why He chose only that widow, He would ask them",If I ask for your last meal, will you be able to give it?"

Solomon is another example in 2 Chronicle 1:6-15:

And Solomon went up thither to the brasen altar before the LORD, which was at the tabernacle of the congregation, and offered a thousand burnt offerings upon it. In that night did God appear unto Solomon, and said unto him, Ask what I shall give thee. And Solomon said unto God, Thou hast shewed great mercy unto David my father, and hast made me to reign in his stead. Now, O LORD God, let thy promise unto David my father be established: for thou hast made me king over a people like the dust of the earth in multitude. Give me now wisdom and knowledge, that I may go out and come in before this people: for who can judge this thy people, that is so great? And God said to Solomon, Because this was in thine heart, and thou hast not asked riches, wealth, or honour, nor the life of thine enemies, neither yet hast asked long life; but hast asked wisdom and knowledge for thyself, that thou mayest judge my people, over whom I have made thee king: Wisdom and knowledge is granted unto thee; and I will give thee riches, and wealth, and honour, such as none of the kings have had that have been before thee, neither shall there any after thee have the like. Then Solomon came from his journey to the high place that was at Gibeon to Jerusalem, from before the tabernacle of the congregation, and reigned over Israel. And Solomon gathered chariots and horsemen: and he had a thousand and four hundred chariots, and twelve thousand horsemen, which he placed in the chariot cities, and with the king at Jerusalem. And the king made silver and gold at Jerusalem as plenteous as stones, and cedar trees made he as the sycomore trees that are in the vale for abundance.

Solomon gave a thousand burnt offerings and God came to him, asking him to ask for anything he wanted. Solomon requested for wisdom, but God added wealth, long life and peace. For a while after I read this scripture for the first time, I wondered why Solomon will only ask God for wisdom. If one is tasty, he will ask for water. If one is hungry, he will ask for food. So, I thought, if Solomon asked for wisdom, it means he realised that he was foolish. But how can a foolish person make such a request? The Holy Spirit resolved this myth for me when he showed me in the Scripture that God set him up because He loved Solomon.

And David comforted Bathsheba his wife, and went in unto her, and lay with her: and she bare a son, and he called his name Solomon: and the LORD loved him. And he sent by the hand of Nathan the prophet; and he called his name Jedidiah, because of the LORD. – 2 Samuel 12:24-25

When Solomon was born, it was David who called him Solomon. The Lord called him Jedidiah, meaning the beloved of the Lord. Do you know that no one can receive anything except it is given him from above?

John answered and said, A man can receive nothing, except it be given him from heaven. – John 3:27

Every good gift and every perfect gift is from above, and cometh down from the Father of

lights, with whom is no variableness, neither shadow of turning. – James 1:17

The Lord said to me that He put the inspiration of giving Him a thousand burnt offerings. Where do you also think He got the inspiration to ask for wisdom? God put it into him. If someone one day asks God, "Why have you not blessed me like Solomon"? God would ask, "Have you given me a thousand burnt offerings before? If I asked you what you desire, would you say it is wisdom? "

When God decides to favour you, he sets you up. He makes you do what no one has ever done before, and then He will swear on you like he did to Abraham, that He will bless you indeed. I believe that picking up this book to read, no matter how it got into your hands is a divine setup! I am confident that the Almighty God before the end of this month will put something in your hands and sa"yG, o ahead; do this one for me", so that before the end of this year, the world will see a difference in your life. If God favours you, the rest will be easy. You will cease to struggle in vain.

The first thing you will ask for is God's grace. The greatest grace that one can receive is the grace of salvation. You must be born again. Let the blood of Jesus wash away all your sins, so that you can enjoy the favour of God. After that, pray the following prayer points that follow with all your heart, asking God to favour you beyond all understanding. Listen carefully to God after these prayers to hear what God will put in your heart to do for Him to set you up for exceeding prosperity.

Prayer Points

1. Father, if you want to favour only one person this year, let it be me, in the name of Jesus.

2. (Bring out an offering/sacrificial seed you have never given before. Hold it up to heaven and say) Father, set me up for a major breakthrough, in the name of Jesus.

3. Oh Lord, put something in my heart to do for you that will open doors of prosperity that no one has ever had, in the name of Jesus.

4. Almighty God, surround me with your favour, in the name of Jesus.

5. Oh Lord, favour me with great testimonies, in the name of Jesus.

6. Lord, use me for your glory so that I will never lack again, in the name of Jesus.

7. Heavenly Father, be gracious unto me from today, in the name of Jesus.

8. In the name of Jesus, the name above all names; I declare that I will never struggle in vain again, in the name of Jesus.

CHAPTER 4: GOD WILL MAKE YOU LAUGH

When the LORD turned again the captivity of Zion, we were like them that dream. Then was our mouth filled with laughter, and our tongue with singing: then said they among the heathen, The LORD hath done great things for them. The LORD hath done great things for us; whereof we are glad.

Turn again our captivity, O LORD, as the streams in the south. They that sow in tears shall reap in joy. He that goeth forth and weepeth, bearing precious seed, shall doubtless come again with rejoicing, bringing his sheaves with him. – Psalm 126

When God prospers you abundantly, it will be as if you are dreaming. His blessings are such that even your enemies will testify that God has blessed you irreversibly. By the time you are done reading this book and applying its principles, you will truly rejoice. The Lord will surely make you laugh!

My emphasis in this chapter shall be in verses 5 and 6 of the above text (Psalm 126):

"They that sow in tears shall reap in joy. He that goeth forth and weepeth, bearing precious seed, shall doubtless come again with rejoicing, bringing his sheaves with him."

The Law of Harvest is a universal law. Galatians 6:7 says:

Be not deceived; God is not mocked: for whatsoever a man soweth, that shall he also reap.

This law holds true whether you are white or black; whether you are a Christian or a Muslim, or never even believes in any God at all. You sow, you reap. However, we also know that the type of soil you sow in will determine the harvest. If the soil is good, the harvest will be good. If the soil is bad, the harvest will be bad.

Basis for Different Levels of Harvest

Supposing that all farmers are sowing in the same type of soil for the same crops; one farmer gets a bountiful harvest (more prosperous), and the other does not. What is responsible? The Bible tells us some of the things that can cause that.

1. Amount of Seed – For example, in 2 Corinthians 9:6 the Bible says,

"But this I say, He which soweth sparingly shall reap also sparingly; and he which soweth bountifully shall reap also bountifully."

If one sowed few seeds, he will surely reap a small harvest. But the one who sowed abundant seed will harvest abundantly.

Supposing that a set of farmers are sowing in the same type of soil, with the same crops in the same amount; why will one prosper and the others lack?

2. Use of Fertilizer – Imagine two farmers who sowed the same crop, in the same soil and the same quantity of seed. The one who uses fertilizers will reap more than the one who did not. What is that fertilizer, you may ask. It is in the same passage above;

"They that sow in tears shall reap in joy. He that goeth forth and weepeth, bearing precious seed, shall doubtless come again with rejoicing, bringing his sheaves with him."

The fertilizer in reaping in joy is not just sowing; it is sowing sacrificially. It is giving in such a way the it causes pain. Sacrificial giving is the fertilizer to reaping in joy.

Sacrificial Giving

In 1 Kings 17:8-16, the widow of Zarephath sowed her last meal. The result was unending harvest. Her pot was full, everyday. In Genesis 22:1-18, God told Abraham to make a sacrifice of his only son, Isaac.

The Bible did not tell us that Abraham wept. But if you were in his shoes, where you had to travel for three days to sacrifice your only son that you love, you will understand how it feels. The pain he felt for going on a three-day journey, knowing that the son of his old age may not return with him must have been unimaginable. What worsened it all was that he was the one who would kill him.

You cannot walk that kind of journey shouting Hallelujah. Abraham wept inwardly. He must have groaned, hoping that in the course of the journey, the Lord will change his mind and speak to him otherwise. But God was quiet, as it happens whenever you sow a seed. You do not hear God immediately you sow a seed. Everything goes into the ground (spiritual soil) and stays quiet. Abraham returned with an irreversible blessing; the Lord swore on him. Not only did he return with an irreversible blessing, he came with multiplication of blessings upon his seed. Sacrificial giving leads to unending and irreversible harvest.

In Mark 12:41-44, the Bible tells of a widow who gave only two mites:

And Jesus sat over against the treasury, and beheld how the people cast money into the

treasury: and many that were rich cast in much. And there came a certain poor widow, and she threw in two mites, which make a farthing. And he called unto him his disciples, and saith unto them, Verily I say unto you, That this poor widow hath cast more in, than all they which have cast into the treasury: For all they did cast in of their abundance; but she of her want did cast in all that she had, even all her living.

The two mites she gave represented 100% of all she had. Her blessing includes the fact that we are talking about her even today. There is a kind of blessing that people cannot keep quiet about.

In 2 Samuel 6:7-12, the Bible records about Obededom:

And the anger of the LORD was kindled against Uzzah; and God smote him there for his error; and there he died by the ark of God. And David was displeased, because the LORD had made a breach upon Uzzah: and he called the name of the place Perezuzzah to this day. And David was afraid of the LORD that day, and said, How shall the ark of the LORD come to me? So David would not remove the ark of the LORD unto him into the city of David: but David carried it aside into the house of Obededom the Gittite. And the ark of the LORD continued in the house of Obededom the Gittite three months: and the LORD blessed Obededom, and all his household. And it was told king David, saying, The LORD hath blessed the house of Obededom, and all that pertaineth unto him, because of the ark of God. So David went and brought up the ark of God from the house of Obededom into the city of David with gladness.

As a result of hosting the ark of the Lord in his house for three months, God blessed Obededom so much that the whole nation was talking about him. This is a similar blessing enjoyed by the widow who gave all she h–ad two mites. Unfortunately, when people want to be stingy; when they do not want to give sacrificially to God, they say they have given their widow's mite. The question I always ask them is, **"Are you a widow? Is this all you have?"**

In 2 Samuel 24:17-24, the Bible tells us about a time when God was angry with David. He asked for forgiveness, asking God to stop killing others and kill him and his family instead. God heard his cry, and instructed him to offer a sacrifice. A man offered to give him all he needed to offer the sacrifice. But David refused to accept offering a sacrifice unto God that did not cost him anything.

And David spake unto the LORD when he saw the angel that smote the people, and said, Lo, I have sinned, and I have done wickedly: but these sheep, what have they done? let thine hand, I pray thee, be against me, and against my father's house. And Gad came that day to David, and said unto him, Go up, rear an altar unto the LORD in the threshingfloor of Araunah the Jebusite. And David, according to the saying of Gad, went up as the LORD commanded. And Araunah looked, and saw the king and his servants coming on toward him: and Araunah went out, and bowed himself before the king on his face upon the ground. And Araunah said, Wherefore is my lord the king come to his servant? And David said, To buy the threshingfloor of thee, to build an altar unto the LORD, that the plague may be stayed from the people. And Araunah said unto David, Let my lord the king take and offer up what seemeth good unto him: behold, here be oxen for burnt sacrifice, and threshing instruments and other instruments of the oxen for wood. All these things did Araunah, as a king, give unto the king. And Araunah said unto the king, The LORD thy God accept thee. And the king said unto Araunah, Nay; but I will surely buy it of thee at a price: neither will I offer burnt offerings unto the LORD my God of that which doth cost me nothing. So David bought the threshingfloor and the oxen for fifty shekels of silver. – 2 Samuel 24:17-24

Sacrificial sowing is the fertilizer for extraordinary harvest. If you sow sacrificially, the harvest will be unending and irreversible. If you sow sacrificially, the harvest will become the talk of the town. If you sow sacrificially, even God's anger against you will be turned away. Those that sow in tears will surely reap in joy.

Spiritual Sowing

Many a time, when we talk about sowing, our mind quickly goes to money. Money is just a part of it. There are other types of sowing. For example, you may have someone precious to you that is not born again. You can begin to sow prayers and fasting for the salvation of their souls, and the knowledge of Jesus Christ. The day that person gives his or her life of Christ, you will reap in joy.

There was a woman who I met many years ago through my best friend. I was the best man of her husband during their wedding. Then she would come to me and preach, telling me to give my life to Christ. I would refute her and tell her that even my name is Enoch – meaning that I was already a Christian by religion. She always wept and prayed for my salvation. Today, she is laughing. The sacrificial seed of prayers that she sowed on the salvation of my soul has yielded increase. Not only should you sow materially, you should sow spiritually – prayers, fasting, witnessing, etc. Those that sow in tears will surely reap in joy.

Prayer Points

1. Lord, let my sorrows be turned into joy, in the name of Jesus.

2. Father, anything that is causing me sorrow, please remove it now, in the name of Jesus.

3. Oh Lord, I am sowing in tears today, let me reap in joy, in the name of Jesus.

4. Father, fill my mouth with laughter, in the name of Jesus.

5. Father, to the glory of your holy name, wipe away poverty from my life this month, in the name of Jesus.

CHAPTER 5: THE INSTRUCTOR

Wisdom is the principal thing; therefore get wisdom: and with all thy getting get understanding. Exalt her, and she shall promote thee: she shall bring thee to honour, when thou dost embrace her. She shall give to thine head an ornament of grace: a crown of glory shall she deliver to thee. – Prov. 4:7-9

Someone once said that we walk by commonsense. In other words, no one teaches a child how to walk. We do not go to school to learn how to work. The child gets up one day, staggers a lot, and eventually starts walking. However, if you want to run competitively, you run by training. If you are going to become an Olympic champion, you will need a coach. You will need someone to train you. Thirdly, we fly by instruction. This is why those who train pilots are called instructors. They are not called teachers, coaches or trainers; they are called instructors.

Commonsense teaches you that you do not plant yam in a river. It tells us that you cannot plant on a rock. Commonsense tells us that the Law of Harvest is real. If you sow abundantly, you will reap abundantly. But if you eat all your harvest and do not plant again, commonsense should tell you that you are likely to go hungry in the coming year. Unfortunately, as it is the case, commonsense is not common. We run by training. We need someone to train us about the types of soil. There are different types of soils, but there are different soil requirements for different crops. One needs to know the right soil to sow in through training. More so, I do not intend to spend much time on running and walking. I am more interested in those that want to fly. Flying is only possible by instruction.

What is Wisdom?

Wisdom is a weapon; just like an arrow. Ecclessiates 7:12 says,

For wisdom is a defence, and money is a defence: but the excellency of knowledge is, that wisdom giveth life to them that have it.

When enemies come around, you use wisdom to chase them away by shooting arrows. Financially, wisdom is superior to money. Proverbs 23:5 has the reason:

Wilt thou set thine eyes upon that which is not? For riches certainly make themselves wings; they fly away as an eagle toward heaven.

If you have money without wisdom, you will soon lose the money. Riches can develop wings and fly away. There is a popular saying that a fool and his money are soon separated. But if you have wisdom and you do not have money, you will soon get money.

Happy is the man that findeth wisdom, and the man that getteth understanding. For the merchandise of it is better than the merchandise of silver, and the gain thereof than fine gold. She is more precious than rubies: and all the things thou canst desire are not to be compared unto her. Length of days is in her right hand; and in her left hand riches and honour. Her ways are ways of pleasantness, and all her paths are peace. She is a tree of life to them that lay hold upon her:

and happy is every one that retaineth her. – Proverbs 3:13-18

If one has wisdom, he will have money, long life, happiness and peace. If you have wisdom, not only will you prosper, you will live long to enjoy it. People will honour you, and you will get peace. The wealth that comes through wisdom is not the type that makes you afraid of the police, the auditor, or financial investigative units.

Wisdom simply means the correct application of knowledge. We apply correct knowledge for our own good. This means that you will first get knowledge, and then use that knowledge correctly. Hosea 4:6 records that God's people are destroyed for the lack of knowledge:

My people are destroyed for lack of knowledge: because thou hast rejected knowledge, I will also reject thee, that thou shalt be no priest to me: seeing thou hast forgotten the law of thy God, I will also forget thy children.

Proverbs 1:5 says that a wise man learns more from what he hears; he gathers knowledge and applies it correctly for his own good.

A wise man will hear, and will increase learning; and a man of understanding shall attain unto wise counsels. – Proverbs 1:5

Interestingly, Proverbs 1:7 declares that fools detest knowledge:

The fear of the LORD is the beginning of knowledge: but fools despise wisdom and instruction.

Because fools lack knowledge, they have nothing to apply or work with. Proverbs 13:20 says:

He that walketh with wise men shall be wise: but a companion of fools shall be destroyed.

In other words, as you walk with the wise, you learn their ways. Your knowledge will increase. Proverbs 9:9 says,

Give instruction to a wise man, and he will be yet wiser: teach a just man, and he will increase in learning.

We see repeatedly that wisdom has to do with acquisition of knowledge, and the correct application of it for our own good. This is what makes wisdom such a powerful weapon.

When God wants to make someone start flying, He begins to give him instructions: "Do this, and this will follo"w.Everybody may hear the same thing, but not everybody will apply what they have heard for their own good. For example, in Luke 6:38, we are instructed to give and then we shall be given:

Give, and it shall be given unto you; good measure, pressed down, and shaken together, and running over, shall men give into your bosom. For with the same measure that ye mete withal it shall be measured to you again. – Luke 6:38

This instruction on giving is not for some people. It is for everybody – sinner, Christian, Muslim, etc. This is what the devil has corrupted with the unbelievers in the form of bribery. The devil knows that when you give, you will get a reward. You do not have to be holy to know how to fly a plane; you simply follow instructions. It works with whosoever is involved.

The Bible gives us yet another instruction in 2 Corinthians 9:6:

But this I say, He which soweth sparingly shall reap also sparingly; and he which soweth bountifully shall reap also bountifully.

This is a strict instruction. We hear it all the time, but only a few apply it. If you ask the elders, they will tell you that those people who go to the devil to get money get strict instructions from the devil to scatter a part of the money. So in parties, some of them spray it, knowing that if they scatter it, they will gather it too.

Another strict instruction is in Jeremiah 17:11:

As the partridge sitteth on eggs, and hatcheth them not; so he that getteth riches, and not by right, shall leave them in the midst of his days, and at his end shall be a fool.

God warns that we must not get money by fraud. This is because if you do, you will not spend it, but will die early. Many people do not pay attention to strict instructions. They do not even learn from those who are more experienced. You will be amazed at how many Christians can quote the story of Gehazi and how he went behind his master to get money and lied (2 Kings 5:20-27). There is hardly any Christian who does not know the story of Judas Iscariot. They know he sold the Lord Jesus Christ for thirsty pieces of silver. They also know that he ended up killing himself.

Recently, I was sharing with our workers in Monrovia that a car can become a moving coffin. If you get money through fraud and use it to buy a car, it becomes a moving coffin. You might be buying your own coffin if you are getting money through any type of fraudulent means. May the type of blessing that brings destruction never come near you in the name of Jesus.

No Christian will say that they do not know about Malachi 3. In fact, we used to joke about it when I was a younger Christian. Some say they love the whole Bible except Malachi 3. We would say jokingly, "Then tear it off your Bible! " If you like, tear that place out of your Bible; it does not remove it from all other millions of copies around the world. This portion of the Bible instructs us that if we do not return our tithe, we attract God's curse into our lives. The question is: Who wants God's curse in his life? Many people hear these things and do not apply them.

Imagine the pains of a father when his child is still crawling when he is supposed to be running. A child like that is called a retarded child. This is how God feels when we are supposed to operate in wisdom and we operating in disobedience or ignorance. I used to question giving of tithe when I was a young Christian, until the Lord told me not to be foolish. I have shared many instructions given to me by God. If God curses you, who will you go to? Some people say that they have not seen the windows of heaven open on them even after returning their tithe. Do you know the type of blessing it is to survive all the economic hardship in the world? You are not even begging bread, lying in the hospital, or hungry. You are not even sick. No one even begs you to eat while others have food but cannot eat.

Proverbs 3:9-10 says another instruction:

Honour the LORD with thy substance, and with the firstfruits of all thine increase: So

shall thy barns be filled with plenty, and thy presses shall burst out with new wine.

You obey instructions if you want to fly. People always shout Hallelujah when you prophecy to them. When you raise prayer points, believers will pray as though their lives depend on it. But when you call for giving, their 'Amen' and 'Halleluiahs' will reduce or even disappear.

It is one thing to have knowledge and another thing to apply it. A teacher cannot teach you all he knows; if not, he may not remain your teacher. But a father will be very willing to teach you all he knows. There are certain secrets that a father will give to his son. God has showed us the secrets to exceeding wealth and greatness. It is now our responsibility to apply them.

When I began to apply instructions from God, my level changed, and has kept changing. God asked me then to double my salary each time I give. God has continued to increase me beyond limits. I gave sacrificially, and I reaped in joy. When you pay your tithe, you have not done anything. It is when you go beyond that that you have started giving. I started practicing it, and until today, God has remained faithful.

I remember a man in Oklahoma, who in a gathering of 17,000 people did something that shocked me. We were raising some money for Kenneth Hagin's ministry. He got up and said that whatever we all contribute is what he and his wife will give. So many people started giving, even more than they wanted just to punish the man. After the collection was calculated, it came to $3,500,000. We were expecting him to probably pass out. But this man asked us, "Brethren, is this all you can do"? This happened in 1979. It was obvious to me that this man knew something that I did not know. I went to him after the program to discover his secret. I found out that he started a business with $500 five years ago, and had an agreement with God to give him 90% of profit and keep 10%. As at the time he was standing before us, $500 had become $50,000,000.

Winning souls is another powerful key to abundance. All your prayers will be supernaturally answered by God. John 15:16 says,

Ye have not chosen me, but I have chosen you, and ordained you, that ye should go and bring forth fruit, and that your fruit should remain: that whatsoever ye shall ask of the Father in my name, he may give it you.

If you bear fruit and your fruit remains, whatever you ask of the Lord, He will do for you. This is why in addition to everything you must have an incurable hunger for soul winning. If you know the way of salvation, and you refuse to show others, you are a dangerous fellow.

Say the following prayers earnestly.

Prayer Points

1. Fathers, let your resurrection power touch my finances today, in the name of Jesus.

2. Father, make me hunger for your knowledge, in the name of Jesus.

3. Oh Lord, give me wisdom to apply the right knowledge I acquire, in the name of Jesus.

4. Oh Lord, remove disobedience from my life, in the name of Jesus.

5. My Father, I receive my breakthrough today, in the name of Jesus.

CHAPTER 6: SECRETS OF ABUNDANCE

I learnt some valuable lessons some years ago. When the crowd of participants at the monthly Holy Ghost service began to increase, I took a critical decision. Because I could no longer handle the crowd singlehandedly, I selected seven elders, and gave them neckties that I had used for the previous ministrations. I told them, "Put on these neckties; they are already soaked with God's anointing during the previous ministrations". Whenever they wore those ties and ministered, supernatural miracles always took place.

Signs and wonders happened at the level of ministrat–ioins spiritual things. All the same, at another level, something else also happened. I was showered with gifts of neckties. Each time people around me travelled, they came back with one type – of gift neckties. If they travelled to South Africa, the only gift they bought for me was neckties. Even if they travelled to America or London, they would bring me neckties. Then I asked the Lord, "Why are these people just giving me neckties? Can't they come up with other gifts besides neckties?"

The Law of Harvest Explained

God gave me an insight into what was happening. He said, "Son, if you sow ties, you will reap ties." I quickly got the message and decided to start sowing shoes. I located pastors who would use the same size of shoes that I wear, and I gave out a good number of shoes, among which were some of my best shoes. I expected a harvest of new ones immediately during the first month, but there were no gifts of shoes for me. When another month rolled by and there were still no gifts of shoes for me, I went to God and said, "Daddy, you told me that if I sow, I would reap." It was then that the Lord taught me another lesson.

He said, "Son, if you plant maize, you can harvest it within three months. But if you plant yam, you will wait a little longer." He continued; "Shoes are greater than ties. The greater the quality of the seed sown, the more time you have to wait for the harvest. You have planted shoes, and you will have to wait a little longer.

But the moment the harvest comes, there will be no stopping."

After a while, I was showered with shoes of all sizes and colours, big shoes, small shoes, white shoes, green shoes, black shoes, and all kinds of sophisticated shoes. When the harvest came in full, I became pleasantly surprised. If you have sown any seed, your harvest will soon come. Just wait a little, and your harvest will locate you in the name of Jesus.

The Place of Honest Work

You must work hard with honesty. If you want to experience unlimited financial breakthrough, you must be prepared for hard and honest work. Many Christians are lazy, but want to prosper. It is quite important to work in order to obtain this level of unlimited prosperity. God may grant you open doors of financial favour, but it will be your responsibility to work towards getting to the pinnacle of financial abundance. To do this, you will be required to do a great deal of hard, smart, and honest work.

The Bible says:

> *But without faith it is impossible to please him: for he that cometh to God must believe that he is, and that he is a rewarder of them that diligently seek him. – Hebrews 11:6*

Diligence in honest work is always rewarded. Farmers work hard to reap bountiful harvest. When they sow seed, they begin to grow. But the mystery of the growing seeds is that weeds also grow side by side. They must then work hard to get rid of the weeds. You are not only expected to work hard, but also pray hard.

Anyone who desires an encounter with the Almighty God, which would cumulate into the unlimited financial breakthrough, you must be ready to work hard and pray hard. The Bible says,

> *I have planted, Apollos watered; but God gave the increase. So then neither is he that planteth any thing, neither he that watereth; but God that giveth the increase. – 1 Corinthians 3:6-7*

Apostle Paul may plant, and Apollos may water. But it is God who gives the increase. You must learn to pray hard and call upon God to give you increase. Lazy people cannot experience unlimited financial breakthrough. Those who are not prepared to work and pray hard are not yet ready for any form of meaningful financial breakthrough.

Put God First

When your harvest begins, you must remember to put God first. The Bible says;

Honor the Lord with your possessions and with the first fruits of all your increase; so your barns will be filled with plenty, and your vats will overflow with new wine. – Proverbs 3: 9-10

The Bible commands that we must honour God with our first fruits. Some people harvest and allow the proceeds to waste away. Until you learn to honour God with your substances, you will not be able to benefit even from the harvest you have laboured to put together. The Bible warns;

Is it time for you, O ye, to dwell in your cieled houses, and this house lie waste? Now therefore thus saith the LORD of hosts; Consider your ways. Ye have sown much, and

bring in little; ye eat, but ye have not enough; ye drink, but ye are not filled with drink; ye clothe you, but there is none warm; and he that earneth wages earneth wages to put it into a bag with holes. Thus saith the LORD of hosts; Consider your ways. Go up to the mountain, and bring wood, and build the house; and I will take pleasure in it, and I will be glorified, saith the LORD. Ye looked for much, and, lo, it came to little; and when ye brought it home, I did blow upon it. Why? saith the LORD of hosts. Because of mine house that is waste, and ye run every man unto his own house. Therefore the heaven over you is stayed from dew, and the earth is stayed from her fruit. And I called for a drought upon the land, and upon the mountains, and upon the corn, and upon the new wine, and upon the oil, and upon that which the ground bringeth forth, and upon men, and upon cattle, and upon all the labour of the hands. – Haggai 1:4-11

Some people gather their harvests and put them in bags with holes. The problem of leaking bags emanates from failure to honour God by giving Him the first fruits of your harvest. If you do not give to God, you may end up wasting away the proceeds of your harvest. Those who harvest into bags with holes are those who refuse to put God first.

Keep Sowing

If you want to experience exceeding greatness as a result of ultimate financial breakthrough, you must keep sowing. The first seed you sow may open the door to blessings, but it takes persistence in sowing to keep the door of blessings open.

For example, look at the story of the widow of Zarephath once again. What opened the door of blessings to her was the first cake she made for Elijah. But what kept the door permanently open was that every day, she kept making cakes for Elijah. Your initial act of giving can take you to a level of financial breakthrough. But what will lead you to the level of unlimited finances is persistent giving. Imagine if by the third day, the widow of Zarephath had stopped giving Elijah food. Then, her source of supply would dry up.

Learn another lesson from Solomon's example. The first time he sacrificed to God, he offered a thousand bullocks in burnt offerings. God prospered him in no small measure. A mighty harvest was unleashed on him. The next time he sacrificed unto God, he offered twenty two thousand oxen.

And Solomon offered a sacrifice of peace offerings, which he offered unto the LORD, two and twenty thousand oxen, and an hundred and twenty thousand sheep. So the king and all the children of Israel dedicated the house of the LORD. – 1 Kings 8:63

Solomon kept increasing in wealth because he kept giving. At the end, he attained the level of unlimited financial greatness. He became so rich that nobody could attempt to count the amount of silver he had.

Unlimited Wealth is Yours

As you read this book, you will become so rich that higher denominations of currencies – one hundred dollars, one thousand naira, and five hundred naira– will be the only denominations of currencies that will matter to you. When your workers bring in the proceeds from your business in cash, you will tell them to hand in the higher denominations and take the lower ones for their benefit.

The mystery behind the giving by the Zarephath widow is uncommon faith in God. It is this type of faith that made her give her only means of sustenance. She gave her only food to Elijah because she needed to surrender the future into the hands of the God of Elijah.

For these secrets of unlimited financial breakthrough to work for you, you must first give your life to Jesus. You must surrender your life to God today if you have not done so already. Today can become your moment of breakthrough. This is your hour of decision.

Prayer Points

1. Father, I hand over my life to you. Take care of my future, in the name of Jesus.

2. [Hold up a special offering as you say this prayer] Father, with this offering, open the door of my prosperity, in the name of Jesus.

3. Father, give me the grace to keep sowing, so that the door of my prosperity will remain open, in the name of Jesus.

4. Father, give me the grace to obey you, no matter how I feel, in the name of Jesus.

5. Father, I receive the grace to work hard, in the name of Jesus.

6. Father, cover me with the garment of prayer, in the name of Jesus.

7. My Father, I move into the realm of exceeding finances, in the name of Jesus.

CHAPTER 7: UNLIMITED FINANCIAL BREAKTHROUGH

And the word of the LORD came unto him, saying, Arise, get thee to Zarephath, which belongeth to Zidon, and dwell there: behold, I have commanded a widow woman there to sustain thee. So he arose and went to Zarephath. And when he came to the gate of the city, behold, the widow woman was there gathering of sticks: and he called to her, and said, Fetch me, I pray thee, a little water in a vessel, that I may drink. And as she was going to fetch it, he called to her, and said, Bring me, I pray thee, a morsel of bread in thine hand. And she said, As the LORD thy God liveth, I have not a cake, but an handful of meal in a barrel, and a little oil in a cruse: and, behold, I am gathering two sticks, that I may go in and dress it for me and my son, that we may eat it, and die.

And Elijah said unto her, Fear not; go and do as thou hast said: but make me thereof a little cake first, and bring it unto me, and after make for thee and for thy son. For thus saith the LORD God of Israel, The barrel of meal shall not waste, neither shall the cruse of oil fail, until the day that the LORD sendeth rain upon the earth. And she went and did according to the saying of Elijah: and she, and he, and her house, did eat many days. And the barrel of meal wasted not, neither did the cruse of oil fail, according to the word of the LORD, which he spake by Elijah. – 1 Kings 17:8-16

The ways of God are very simple. Biblical principles enable us to achieve unusual breakthroughs with ease. There are breakthroughs, and there are unlimited breakthroughs. When we talk about the unlimited breakthrough, we refer to the breakthrough that swallows up all other breakthroughs.

God can give you what I term "The Unlimited Breakthrough." He can take your finances to realm where the thoughts of poverty will be completely banished from your life. It is God's intention to pour on his sons and daughters, the unlimited financial breakthrough.

Revealed Secrets

God has raised several multimillionaires through the monthly "Divine Encounter" Program of our church. This is why the main objective of this book is to lay bare before you, the secrets of unlimited financial breakthrough. Its pages contain uncommon exposition of wisdom, which will lead you to the peak of financial breakthrough. God is not interested in leading you to minimal breakthroughs. He wants to take you to the peak. The secrets of explosive financial breakthrough can be summed up in this sentence; "Knowing what to do to get the best results, and doing it."

The story of the widow of Zarephath aptly illustrates this principle also. The widow was told what to do, and she carried out the instructions given her.

What Must I Do?

If there is any question jumping around in your head it "isW, hat must I do to prosper, and get to the level of unlimited prosperity"? The story of the widow of Zarephath answers the question. You can move from zero to hero. You may start from the most humble beginning, and still reach the peak of financial sufficiency. In other words, the poorest can become the richest. The man who lives from hand to mouth can be made to become a benefactor to hundreds and thousands of people.

I am yet to come across someone that is as poor as the widow in question. She was so poor that she had only one meal left in her life. From zero point, the Almighty God took her to a point where she never lacked again. Likewise, I decree upon your life as you read this book, you will be so enriched that you will be able to feed a whole city, in the name of Jesus!

Divine Principles of Abundance

There are some principles derived from the story of the widow of Zarephath. These principles, tested and proven, are God's blueprint for securing unlimited financial breakthrough. If you follow them, you will move from the present level of your finances to the peak of financial freedom and sufficiency. God will so shower you with abundant financial resources that besides being comfortable, you will begin to finance projects in the church and your community. You will move from the level of those who manage meager resources to the class of those who eat what they want, buy what they want, live comfortably, and meet the needs of others.

In this world of economic recession and scarce resources, it is possible to become a candidate of divine outpouring. The Almighty can locate you and make you a recipient of unlimited financial breakthrough. All you need is to follow these Principles:

1. Sow When it is Practically Difficult to Do-STohe widow of Zarephath sowed when it was absolutely inconvenient for her to do so, because, she sowed the last thing she had. It is quite easy to give part of your excesses, and it is simple to give out of what you no longer need. But the giver who is going to be specially blessed by God is the one who gives when it hurts.

The level of giving is not measured by what is given, but by what is left after one has given. A lot of people cast offerings when Jesus was at the temple, but the Lord singled out only a particular widow. The widow did not give much, but because she gave all that she had, Jesus declared her to be the greatest giver.

And Jesus sat over against the treasury, and beheld how the people cast money into the treasury: and many that were rich cast in much. And there came a certain poor widow, and she threw in two mites, which make a farthing. And he called unto him his disciples, and saith unto them, Verily I say unto you, That this poor widow hath cast more in, than all they which have cast into the treasury: For all they did cast in of their abundance; but she of her want did cast in all that she had, even all her living. – Mark 12:41-44

This widow had no husband to provide for her. Her husband must have died and left nothing behind. Hence, she became a poor widow. A mite is the smallest Jewish coin valued at about fourth of an American cent. What she gave was so materially insignificant.

This kind of giving was also done by the Corinthian believers who gave in spite of their poverty.

How that in a great trial of affliction the abundance of their joy and their deep poverty abounded unto the riches of their liberality.

For to their power, I bear record, yea, and beyond their power they were willing of themselves. – 2 Corinthians 8:2-3

Even if you are poor today, God can make you richer than the richest man in your community. If you can learn and practice the type of giving exemplified by the widow, you can give your way to prosperity by offering the type of gifts which provokes God. If widows can give all they have, why can people who are better positioned in life not give more? God is looking for sacrificial givers; those who will give even when it is not convenient.

Every man according as he purposeth in his heart, so let him give; not grudgingly, or of necessity: for God loveth a cheerful giver. – 2 Corinthians 9:7

If you want to challenge God with giving, give when it is not convenient, and God will be forced to bless you in an extraordinary manner. Solomon laid bare the secrets of his success and wealth in the passage below:

He that observeth the wind shall not sow; and he that regardeth the clouds shall not reap. As thou knowest not what is the way of the

spirit, nor how the bones do grow in the womb of her that is with child: even so thou knowest not the works of God who maketh all. In the morning sow thy seed, and in the evening withhold not thine hand: for thou knowest not whether shall prosper, either this or that, or whether they both shall be alike good. – Ecclesiastes 11:4-6

Here, we discover the secrets of Solomon's abundant wealth. He was an incurable giver. You can be one too if you do not wait until it is convenient to give. Sow in the morning, in the afternoon, and in the evening. Keep on sowing and God will keep on blessing you.

2. Sow on Good Ground– The widow of Zarephath sowed on a very good ground. Sowing on good ground is illustrated by the parable of the sower and the seed.

Hearken; Behold, there went out a sower to sow: And it came to pass, as he sowed, some fell by the way side, and the fowls of the air came and devoured it up. And some fell on stony ground, where it had not much earth; and immediately it sprang up, because it had no depth of earth: But when the sun was up, it was scorched; and because it had no root, it withered away. And some fell among thorns, and the thorns grew up, and choked it, and it yielded no fruit. And other fell on good ground, and did yield fruit that sprang up and increased; and brought forth, some thirty, and some sixty, and some an hundred. – Mark 4:3-8

Here the Bible tells us that there are various grounds to sow on. The type of ground you sow would determine your yield or output. The widow of Zarephath sowed on the best ground. She had one seed to sow, yet she knew that where she sowed the seed matters, and would go a long way to determining her harvest. She identified a very fertile ground and sowed on it.

The unwise sow by the roadside, among the thorns and on stony grounds. The wise on the other hand, ensure that they sow on good soil. Those who sow on good grounds would come up with three categories of harvest:

- The thirty-fold harvest
- The sixty-fold harvest
- The hundred-fold harvest

The type of harvest which achieves results can be classified into the above three categories. The thirty-fold return is secured by those who give to members of the household of faith.

And let us not be weary in well doing: for in due season we shall reap, if we faint not. As we have therefore opportunity, let us do good unto all men, especially unto them who are of the household of faith. – Galatians 6:9-10

Each gift you offer to the brethren will attract the thirty-fold return. The sixty-fold return is achieved when you give to pastors, prophets, evangelists, and other men and women of God.

He that receiveth a prophet in the name of a prophet shall receive a prophet's reward; and he that receiveth a righteous man in the name of a righteous man shall receive a righteous man's reward. – Matthew 10:41

To achieve the hundred-fold return, you have to give to the high priest. In this regard, you are not expected to give to the prophet, but to give to the head of the sons of the prophets.

The widow of Zarephath sowed into the life of Elijah. Thus, she was able to key into the source of superfluous blessings as she reaped a hundred-fold return. She did not only get food to eat for the rest of her life, but she also had death expelled when it was trying to kill her only child. When you sow into the life of a high priest, you do not only get monetary returns, you also get what money cannot buy.

Be a Wise Giver

Let me share some striking testimonies with you. A young man once walked into my office and said," Daddy, I want to give you a house." I gave him a tense answe"rI: don't need your house. I already have my own hous"e.Because I live in the Redemption Camp, I explained to him that I do not need a house in the city, where the house gift was located. The man insisted that I must receive the gift, but I refused.

In his bid to convince me, he told me that he had two houses and that offering to give me one was great. I told him that I know some pastors who would gladly receive such a gift. I even offered to give him their names. But he insisted that I must accept this house by all means. When I saw his unyielding resolve, I told him to go home, pray, and return after three months.

Three months later, he came back and said," Daddy, I have prayed and I'm convinced that God wants me to give you the house. The keys are here." I prayed and asked God to tell me what to do. God told me to accept the gift, and I did. In the course of making enquiries, I discovered that one of the branches of the Redeemed Christian Church of God needed an accommodation in the same vicinity of that house. So I willingly offered them the facility to use for Church Services.

Within a short while, the man came back with a request, he asked, "Daddy will you kindly accept to go somewhere wit"h me? I obliged. He took me to a place where there was a very big estate. Beaming with smiles, the young man said,"Daddy, this is what the Lord has done for me. I want you to dedicate this estate to His glory!" Displaying a fatherly sense of humour I said", Young man, you must be smart. You gave God a house and you got an estate."

If the young man had held unto his house, he would not have come anywhere near becoming someone who owns an estate.

Divine Intervention

A particular sister took up the responsibility of attending to my needs during my visits to a town in Western Nigeria. During one of those visits, I met the sister where she parked her car, but she was in a very sad mood. I questioned in my mind why she stood beside her car in that mood. Initially, I thought her car had developed a problem, but she replied, **"Daddy, nothing is wrong with the car, but something is wrong with me."**

She had suffered a miscarriage. An eight-month old foetus died in her womb, and doctors were planning to flush out the dead foetus. She stood there sorrowful and depressed. I laid hands on her womb and called on the Almighty God to intervene. Few minutes later, the baby came back to life and God restored unto the sister what the enemy had stolen from her. The same God who gave life to a dead baby in the womb will visit you with His resurrection power today, in the name of Jesus.

Prayer Points

1. Father, give me the grace to give even when it is very difficult, in the name of Jesus

2. Dear Father, give me the spirit of discernment to know the right soil to sow, in the name of Jesus.

3. Father, as I sow, I shall receive my harvest, in the name of Jesus.

4. Father, let your resurrection power fall on my finances, in the name of Jesus.

5. Father, cause every power holding onto my harvest to vomit it by fire, in the name of Jesus.

6. Oh Lord, let me not eat my seed that I am supposed to sow, in the name of Jesus.

7. Oh Lord, help me not to get tired of giving, in the name of Jesus

8. Father, as I give, launch me into the realm of unlimited financial breakthrough, in the name of Jesus.

CHAPTER 8: GREAT EXPECTATION

And the word of the LORD came unto him, saying, Arise, get thee to Zarephath, which belongeth to Zidon, and dwell there: behold, I have commanded a widow woman there to sustain thee. So he arose and went to Zarephath. And when he came to the gate of the city, behold, the widow woman was there gathering of sticks: and he called to her, and said, Fetch me, I pray thee, a little water in a vessel, that I may drink. And as she was going to fetch it, he called to her, and said, Bring me, I pray thee, a morsel of bread in thine hand. And she said, As the LORD thy God liveth, I have not a cake, but an handful of meal in a barrel, and a little oil in a cruse: and, behold, I am gathering two sticks, that I may go in and dress it for me and my son, that we may eat it, and die. And Elijah said unto her, Fear not; go and do as thou hast said: but make me thereof a little cake first, and bring it unto me, and after make for thee and for thy son. For thus saith the LORD God of Israel, The barrel of meal shall not waste, neither shall the cruse of oil fail, until the day that the LORD sendeth rain upon the earth. And she went and did according to the saying of Elijah: and she, and he, and her house, did eat many days. And the barrel of meal wasted not, neither did the cruse of oil fail, according to the word of the LORD, which he spake by Elijah. – 1 Kings 17:8-16

The widow of Zarephath had great expectation because she was chosen for divine visitation. She was selected for a divine encounter. Luke 4:25-26 states:

But I tell you of a truth, many widows were in Israel in the days of Elias, when the heaven was shut up three years and six months, when great famine was throughout all the land; But unto none of them was Elias sent, save unto Sarepta, a city of Sidon, unto a woman that was a widow.

There were many widows in the land in her time that needed a miracle, but God singled her out for a divine encounter. I believe God that as you read this book, He will single you out for a divine encounter.

The widow of Zarephath had geat expectations because of some reasons:

She Knew God's Ways

This widow must have been aware of what happens when God visits. They all had read the first five books of Moses to find out the accounts of Abraham. Every time God visits a people, He turns things around. In Genesis 18, when God visited Abraham and his family, his sorrow turned into laughter. So, this widow must have heard about it. Even in Genesis 19, when God paid Lot a visit, a divine encounter, Lot's family was delivered from destruction. Somehow she knew she was facing a difficult situation, but God had chosen to pay her a visit. She said,"Without any doubt, all will be well." I also believe God for you, that without doubt all will be well in your future and finances.

God Has Spoken

The second reason she had a great expectation is that God had spoken. The man of God said, "...Thus saith the Lord..". God had spoken. The word of God once spoken is settled. As stated in Psalm 33:8-9,

Let all the earth fear the LORD: let all the inhabitants of the world stand in awe of him. For he spake, and it was done; he commanded, and it stood fast.

God had spoken, not just to the widow, but also to the barrel and bottle of oil. She knew that when God speaks, even your pocket will hear. So when God said*"From now on, there will be no lack in this home,"* she believed. Do you believe that from now on, you will never know poverty again?

Yea, before the day was I am he; and there is none that can deliver out of my hand: I will work, and who shall let it? – Isaiah 43:13

When God wants to work, no one can hinder him. If He singles you out for favour, no one can do anything about it. I am telling you right now that anyone who wants to stand in your way of success will not see the New Year, in the mighty name of Jesus Christ. This is because if God wants to work, anyone who stands in his way will be crushed. Man is grass, and all his beauty is like flower that fades. Therefore if God wants to work for you and the Red Sea suddenly says "no," all He has to do is breath, and there will be a way where no way ever existed before.

Beginning from this moment, where there is no way for you, there will be a way, in the mighty name of our Lord Jesus Christ.

God's Prophet has Spoken

Elijah said, "Thus saith the Lord..". The widow believed. In verse 16 of our key scripture, it is recorded that it happened as the Lord spoke through his Prophet, Elijah. Believing in the words of God's prophet brings prosperity.

And they rose early in the morning, and went forth into the wilderness of Tekoa: and as they went forth, Jehoshaphat stood and said, Hear me, O Judah, and ye inhabitants of Jerusalem; Believe in the LORD your God, so shall ye be established; believe his prophets, so shall ye prosper. – 2 Chronicles 20:20

I speak to you as God's oracle and prophet: In a way you can never understand, you will prosper. In the name that is above every other name, JESUS; from now on, ways shall be opened unto you. Where you have failed before; beginning from now, you will succeed, in the name of Jesus.

In 1 Samuel 3:19, God vowed never to allow the word of his prophet to fall to the ground:

And Samuel grew, and the LORD was with him, and did let none of his words fall to the ground.

I have told this story so many times. I know a man who was so poor. In fact, between me and him, I could not tell who was poorer. I was led by the Holy Spirit to give him the savings I had to start a business. I told him that the money will never finish. Today, I can count at least two houses he owns that can be truly called mansions.

That is because the money as I prophesied never finished. I prophesy to you today that whatever is left in your pocket now will never finish, in Jesus' name.

Awareness of the Unchanging Law of Harvest

This widow knew about the unchanging law of harvest. She knew that Genesis 8:22 that,

While the earth remaineth, seedtime and harvest, and cold and heat, and summer and winter, and day and night shall not cease.

As long as the earth remains, seedtime and harvest shall never cease. She knew it is God's word, and therefore is settled forever. She understood that if she sows she will reap. Harvest only comes when you have sowed.

The problem with many of us is that when what we have is little, we want to hold on to it. If you do not sow, how will it produce a harvest? I remember some time ago when I was still struggling. We had just one tuber of yam left in the whole house. Someone came to visit us, and my wife in her usual way does not allow people leave our house empty handed. She gave out that tuber of yam. I almost said (although I never said it out)", Darling, Jesus said if you have two coats, give out one…" But here was only one tuber of yam, and she gave it out. But according to the law of harvest, before that day was over, our house was full of yams!

This widow also realized that the law of harvest works in proportion. The more you sow, the more you reap. Also, the less you sow, the less you reap.

But this I say, He which soweth sparingly shall reap also sparingly; and he which soweth bountifully shall reap also bountifully. – 2 Cor 9:6

She was aware that the one who sows all will reap all. All she had was what the man of God asked for, but she knew it was a seed and gave it. She must have also read in Genesis 22, where God asked Abraham to give him his all– Isaac. Abraham was willing to let go. After he passed the test, the Almighty God promised to bless him and multiply his seed.

This widow was chosen among so many widows. She was not even a Jew or one we could call a Christian in our time. Why would God choose her?

Well, in Psalm 115:3 says*",But our God is in the heavens: he hath done whatsoever he hath please"d*. God does not need permission from anyone to do what He intends doing. God does not ask your neighbour or friends before He chooses you. God is sovereign and does what he pleases. However, God is not arbitrary. God knew there was something in that woman that the moment she hears the name of God, she will respond.

I love them that love me; and those that seek me early shall find me. – Proverbs 8:7

If you love God, He will love you. The moment she heard it was God requesting for her last meal, she said, "You can have it!"

The million dollar question is: Who will God choose? The choice is yours.

The Almighty God knows all of us crying to him for one breakthrough or another. He knows those who will spend their breakthrough on themselves alone. He also knows those who will use it for his glory – he knows all these from what we do with what we have now. God knows us inside out.

The Almighty God is looking for divine treasurers. He is looking for someone who will say", Whatever you put in my hands, you can have it." He is looking to pick someone for an unlimited financial divine encounter. Will you be the one?

Prayer Points

1. Father, if you need a divine treasurer, I am here. I will serve you with all I have for the rest of my life.

2. Father, if you want to choose someone for a divine visitation, I am available. Use me for your glory, in the name of Jesus.

3. Father, even as you are blessing me, bless my family and friends also, in the name of Jesus.

4. Father, do marvellous things for me, in the name of Jesus.

5. Father, put an end to poverty in my life, in the name of Jesus.

6. Father, open great divine doors for me, in the name of Jesus.

7. Father, exceed my expectations, in the name of Jesus.

8. Father, if you are going to use only one person this season, let it be me, in the name of Jesus.

9. Father, even with the little I have I want to demonstrate that I love you. Bless me, in Jesus' name.

10. Father, open the floodgates of blessings unto me, in the name of Jesus.

CHAPTER 9: THE KEYS OF DAVID

I will bless the LORD at all times: his praise shall continually be in my mouth. My soul shall make her boast in the LORD: the humble shall hear thereof, and be glad. O magnify the LORD with me, and let us exalt his name together. – Psalm 34:1-3

If you are looking for someone who rose from grass to grace, you cannot get a better example than David. If you are looking for someone who succeeded beyond human expectation do not look further; look at David. If you are looking for someone who was unknown; someone who was forgotten; someone who among his brethren did not count; he became the head of a nation. If you are looking for someone who started as a nobody, but even today has his name ringing all over the universe; look for somebody called David. If you are looking for someone who was a shepherd boy, but who Jesus is addressed as his son; look for David.

Jesus rejoiced to be called 'The Son of David'. You need to find out what is the secret of the fellow called David. What is it that he had or knew that changed his life completely? What was the key of David? We sincerely need to find out. This is because the moment we can find out the secret of David, our way to success is guaranteed.

David's Secret

Taking a closer look at the key text above, you will have an idea what the secret of David was. He says", I will bless the Lord at all times: his praise will continually be in my mouth ...

David was saying that he would only boast of no other thing but the Lord. He continues to say that everybody will hear him boasting about the goodness, the mercy, the greatness, the power, the generosity of His God, and they would fear. He then looked at all others and wished they knew what he knew and joined him in exalting the name of God together.

David made a great discovery that anything you want to get from God; anywhere you want to get to in life; anything you need to get done; if only you can learn this one secret you will su–cceed Praising the Lord!

In Psalm 103:1 David also says, **"Bless the LORD, O my soul: and all that is within me, bless his holy name"**. He meant his heart, his kidney, his intestine, his lungs, his stomach, his blood, his water... all that is within him, must bless God's holy name!

David says in another place in Psalm 108:1, **"O God, my heart is fixed; I will sing and give praise, even with my glory.**" His heart is fixed like concrete that is set. When you pour concrete and it is still wet, you can push it around. But once it is set, it is set forever. David says here that his heart is fixed within him to bless the Lord. This means that his heart was set as concrete upon the Lord. What surrender!

David confirms this in another place in Psalm 122:1, **"I was glad when they said unto me, Let us go into the house of the** *LORD.*" He did not say he was glad because they asked him to come and receive millions of dollars. It was not because they asked David to come and sign a new juicy contract. He was glad only because they asked him to go to the house of God.

In Psalm 27:4 David says,

One thing have I desired of the LORD, that will I seek after; that I may dwell in the house of the LORD all the days of my life, to behold the beauty of the LORD, and to enquire in his temple.

David's only prayer request was to dwell in God's house forever, and behold his glory. One day he was dancing for God, already a king. He danced so mightily that his belly came out of his dress. His wife wondered, "Your majesty, look at the way you were dancing; disgracing yourself in public". David replied her by saying, "of whom was I dancing for? Is it not the God who took me from nothing and enthroned me as king over Israel ahead of your Father, Saul?"

David recalled that it was the Lord who took him from zero to glory; the one who gave him the greatest breakthrough he could ever have.

David gave everything he had, including himself to God. Even if no one else wanted to worship God, David vowed to bless the Lord at all times. If we beak this down it means: In the morning I will bless God. In the afternoon, I will bless the Lord. In the evening,

I will bless the Lord. Even when I wake up in the night, I will bless the Lord. When I am eating, I will bless the Lord. When I am fighting, I will bless you. Everywhere I go I will bless you. In everything I do, I will bless you. He says",...your praise will continually be in my mouth." Breaking it down further it means: I will never grumble; I will never complain; no one will ever hear me asking", Why is this happening to me"? This is what it means when God's praise is continually in your mouth.

One day, David's father, Jesse, asked him to take food to his brothers who were fighting a battle. There he met a giant called Goliath, boasting and defying the God of Israel. So he wondered, "This man is not praising God. That is bad enough. But if he opens his mouth again to defy my God. Goliath, you are dead!" Everyone, including his elder brothers warned him to go back home, but he refused. Even King Saul told him that he had no amour or weapons, but he insisted to fight a fully armed giant with stones! To David, it was about the name of God. He would rather die than see anyone insult God the way Goliath did. So David thought, "Even if he kills me, I will not let him continue to insult my God!"

One day David woke up and thought about what he could do for God. So he said to himself, "I have an idea." He sent for the priest. When the priest arrived, he told him", I want to build a house for the Lord alone. Please don't let anyone know. I want to do it alone." The priest said, "go ahead." But on his way the Lord spoke to the prophet and told him that David's hands were filled with blood as a warrior, and so, could not build him a temple. However, God asked that David's Son, who would rule after him, build the temple. The prophet returned and broke the message to David. David did not argue. He surrendered to God's will.

So David says to his son", Congratulations! God said you are the one who will build the temple. I won't let you spend anything. I will provide every material you will ever need to build the temple." What a man!

When we compare ourselves to David; when we place ourselves side by side with him, we are brought to tears. When we say we love God, and we have to be begged to return your tithe and give your offerings. This man, David says, "Since you won't let me build you a house, Lord, no one will contribute to the resources, I will provide it alone". Little wonder the Almighty God looked down from heaven and vowed that there would always be someone from the house of David, sitting on the throne. Always!

Do you want a divine encounter; the kind that will never be forgotten? Do you want to be one of the few that the world will never forget? Then learn from David.

Years ago when we started what we called the **Christ Redeemer's Congress**, I would gather school children and adults who want to come to a Grammar School with boarding houses. We fed and accommodated them for free. We had no money. I was probably the richest one among my crew, still using a second hand car. But I had some people with me who loved God passionately. On one occasion, we needed money for the Congress. One woman submitted her whole salary for the month. She was working in Lagos Island, but lived in Surulere. I wondered how she would cope. She said she will trek to work to and fro. 'God has a need' she said, 'And so my need is secondary'. Today, the woman is unbelievably wealthy.

I feel ashamed when people have to wait to be cajoled to give a reasonable offering unto God. Do you realize the offering is to the One who saved your soul from hell, and made you a candidate of heaven? If someone will spend ten minutes begging you to give to the One who gave His only Son to save you, then there is a problem.

If you want to experience unlimited greatness, learn from David. Live a life of praise to God. Worship God always with all that you have. Give all that you have, including yourself to God and watch him catapult you from zero to unlimited greatness.

Praise Points

In this chapter, you will not pray to ask God for anything. You will praise him NON-STOP for as many hours as you can. Use these praise points in your section of praise.

1. Lord, I magnify you. Let everything within me praise the Lord.

2. Father, I pour out everything in me at your feet to praise you.

3. Blessed be the name of the Lord forever.

4. Lord, I will praise you and my heart will boast in you.

5. I will tell everyone how good, glorious, and merciful you are.

6. I will tell the world of the Lord who brought me out of darkness into His marvellous light.

7. I will bless the one who died that I may live.

8. I will praise the one who was rejected by the Father on the cross that I may be accepted.

9. I will bless the Lord at all times; his praise will be in my mouth continually.

10. Oh Lord, you are worthy of my praise and adoration. My Unchangeable Changer.

CHAPTER 10: THE SECRETS OF GREAT SEEDS

And the angel of the LORD called unto Abraham out of heaven the second time, And said, By myself have I sworn, saith the LORD, for because thou hast done this thing, and hast not withheld thy son, thine only son: That in blessing I will bless thee, and in multiplying I will multiply thy seed as the stars of the heaven, and as the sand which is upon the sea shore; and thy seed shall possess the gate of his enemies; And in thy seed shall all the nations of the earth be blessed; because thou hast obeyed my voice. –
Genesis 22:15-18

In this chapter, we will be talking about the secret of great seeds; the secrets of seeds that became great; the secrets of children who become far, far greater than their fathers.

Abraham and Isaac

The Almighty God promised to make Abraham great.

Now the LORD had said unto Abram, Get thee out of thy country, and from thy kindred, and from thy father's house, unto a land that I will shew thee: And I will make of thee a great nation, and I will bless thee, and make thy name great; and thou shalt be a blessing: And I will bless them that bless thee, and curse him that curseth thee: and in thee shall all families of the earth be blessed. – Genesis 12:1-3

The Bible records that Abraham eventually became great. In Genesis 13, we see a glimpse of his greatness.

And Abram was very rich in cattle, in silver, and in gold. – Genesis 13:2

By Genesis 24:34-35 it is recorded that God had made Abraham great as He promised. This was the testimony of Abraham's servant.

And he said, I am Abraham's servant. And the LORD hath blessed my master greatly; and he is become great: and he hath given him flocks, and herds, and silver, and gold, and

menservants, and maidservants, and camels, and asses. – Genesis 24:34-35

In Genesis 26 we discover that as great as Abraham was, Isaac, his son, was greater.

Then Isaac sowed in that land, and received in the same year an hundredfold: and the LORD blessed him. And the man waxed great, and went forward, and grew until he became very great: For he had possession of flocks, and possession of herds, and great store of servants: and the Philistines envied him. – Genesis 26:12-14

Abraham was great, but Isaac was very great. He was greater than his father. In the name of Jesus, you will be greater than your parents, and your children will be greater than you.

The important question here is: What is the secret? How come Abraham was great and Isaac was greater? A careful study of the entire chapter of Genesis 22, where God tested Abraham to sacrifice his son Isaac to Him is very important. Isaac was the only son Abraham loved. But he obeyed God and tied him up for sacrifice. God stopped him and provided an animal for the sacrifice. Therefore, God swore that in blessing, he would bless Abraham. But in multiplying, he would multiply his seed. This means that Abraham would get the blessing and his seed would get a multiplication of the blessing he carried.

Isaac was Abraham's best. He was his first fruit. Proverbs 3:9-10 records God's command for us to give him our first fruit.

Honour the LORD with thy substance, and with the firstfruits of all thine increase: So shall thy barns be filled with plenty, and thy presses shall burst out with new wine.

God saw Abraham giving him his first fruit and swore to bless him and multiply his generations. Concerning blessing Abraham, his blessings would be irreversible. The story of Abraham included Ishmael, but he had sent him away. Isaac surrendered his life to be slain for sacrifice unto God. Whereas Abraham gave his best (the son he loved most out of two), Isaac gave his all. After all, if that knife in Abraham's hand had come down, Isaac would not have another life.

Remember the story in Mark 12:41-44 of the widow who gave out of nothing.

And Jesus sat over against the treasury, and beheld how the people cast money into the treasury: and many that were rich cast in much. And there came a certain poor widow, and she threw in two mites, which make a farthing. And he called unto him his disciples, and saith unto them, Verily I say unto you, That this poor widow hath cast more in, than all they which have cast into the treasury: For all they did cast in of their abundance; but she of her want did cast in all that she had, even all her living. – Mark 12:41-44

Jesus taught us again that the other rich men gave out of abundance. But the poor widow gave her all. Such was the case of Isaac. He gave his all. Here lies the secret of the seed that is greater than their parents: Whereas the parents give their best, their seed give their all.

David and Solomon

Another example of a seed that was greater than his parent is the case of David and Solomon. The Bible records that David was very rich.

Furthermore David the king said unto all the congregation, Solomon my son, whom alone God hath chosen, is yet young and tender, and the work is great: for the palace is not for man, but for the LORD God. Now I have prepared with all my might for the house of my God the gold for things to be made of gold, and the silver for things of silver, and the brass for things of brass, the iron for things of iron, and wood for things of wood; onyx stones, and stones to be set, glistering stones, and of divers colours, and all manner of precious stones, and marble stones in abundance. Moreover, because I have set my affection to the house of my God, I have of mine own proper good, of gold and silver, which I have given to the house of my God, over and above all that I have prepared for the holy house, Even three thousand talents of gold, of the gold of Ophir, and seven thousand talents of refined silver, to overlay the walls of the houses withal: The gold for things of gold, and the silver for things of silver, and for all manner of work to be made

by the hands of artificers. And who then is willing to consecrate his service this day unto the LORD? – 1 Chronicles 29:1-5

When David was not allowed to build a house of the Lord, he supplied all the money for the building of the temple: Three thousand talents of gold and seven thousand talents of refined silver and other precious stones and items. Bible scholars tell us that compared to our modern times, what David gave was in billions of dollars. You must be rich to build a temple alone and spend billions of dollars.

However, Solomon became greater than his father, David. He was the richest man on earth in his days. 2 Chronicles 1 records that Solomon was so rich that silver and gold were like ordinary stones.

And the king made silver and gold at Jerusalem as plenteous as stones, and cedar trees made he as the sycomore trees that are in the vale for abundance. – 2 Chronicles 1:15

Whenever people brought silver to Solomon, he would probably ask them to dump them at the backyard. Gold was the minimum item Solomon had in his house.

What then is the difference between David and Solomo-n father and son? David gave massively, but Solomon gave what no one had ever given before. 2 Chronicles records what he gave to the Lord.

And Solomon went up thither to the brasen altar before the LORD, which was at the tabernacle of the congregation, and offered a thousand burnt offerings upon it. In that night did God appear unto Solomon, and said unto him, Ask what I shall give thee. And Solomon said unto God, Thou hast shewed great mercy unto David my father, and hast made me to reign in his stead. Now, O LORD God, let thy promise unto David my father be established: for thou hast made me king over a people like the dust of the earth in multitude. Give me now wisdom and knowledge, that I may go out and come in before this people: for who can judge this thy people, that is so great?

And God said to Solomon, Because this was in thine heart, and thou hast not asked riches, wealth, or honour, nor the life of thine enemies, neither yet hast asked long life; but hast asked wisdom and knowledge for thyself, that thou mayest judge my people, over whom I have made thee king: Wisdom and knowledge is granted unto thee; and I will give thee riches, and wealth, and honour, such as none of the kings have had that have been before thee, neither shall there any after thee have the like.

Then Solomon came from his journey to the high place that was at Gibeon to Jerusalem, from before the tabernacle of the congregation, and reigned over Israel. And Solomon gathered chariots and horsemen: and he had a thousand and four hundred chariots, and twelve thousand horsemen, which he placed in the chariot cities, and with the king at Jerusalem.

And the king made silver and gold at Jerusalem as plenteous as stones, and cedar trees made he as the sycomore trees that are in the vale for abundance. And Solomon had horses brought out of Egypt, and linen yarn:

the king's merchants received the linen yarn at a price. And they fetched up, and brought forth out of Egypt a chariot for six hundred shekels of silver, and an horse for an hundred and fifty: and so brought they out horses for all the kings of the Hittites, and for the kings of Syria, by their means. – 2 Chronicles 1:6-17

Before Solomon, no one had ever given more than seven burnt offerings to the Lord. He gave what made God not keep quiet. When the priests slew the seventh offering, they thought they were there already. But Solomon ordered them to continue. And then they got to twenty. They started wondering what the king was thinking. And they got to one hundred, two hundred, three hundred; they would have thought in their mind"sY, our majesty, are you ok?" They had not seen anything yet, as Solomon went all the way to one thousand blessed burnt offering to the King of all kings!

As a result of what Solomon did, God blessed him exceeding–ly because he did what no one had done before, God made him somebody that no one had ever been. If Solomon had stopped there, it would have been ok. After God had blessed him, he returned unto God an offering that no one has ever been able to beat. He went on to break his own record in 2 Chronicles 7.

And king Solomon offered a sacrifice of twenty and two thousand oxen, and an hundred and twenty thousand sheep: so the king and all the people dedicated the house of God. – 2 Chronicles 7:5

How long would it have taken them to slaughter the animals one after another - twenty two thousand cows and one hundred and twenty thousand sheep? No wonder Solomon is in a class of his own.

One day, I read an article about cars. They were comparing different cars and their usability. They classified BMW as the fastest; Mercedes as the strongest; Lexus as the most comfortable, and so on. So I told the people around me, "But I have driven in all these types of cars." Then I asked, "What about Rose Royce?" They replied, "Daddy, leave Rose Royce alone. It is in a class of its own". So is Solomon in his own class among all the wealthy people that existed. Such shall be your case if wealthy people in the world are compared in our time, in the name of Jesus.

Proverbs 22:6 says,

Train up a child in the way he should go: and when he is old, he will not depart from it.

Do you want your seed to be greater than you? Teach that child to give more than you can ever give. Teach them from cradle and it will not leave them. It is not just by telling the children, but showing them by your examples. This is because there is only one way to unlimited financial breakthrough – sacrificial giving.

Proverbs 11:24-25 says,

There is that scattereth, and yet increaseth; and there is that withholdeth more than is meet, but it tendeth to poverty. The liberal soul shall be made fat: and he that watereth shall be watered also himself.

Show your child to be greater than you by the way you give to the Lord liberally. Children learn from what they can see much more than what they hear. I want you to become uniquely prosperous.

Something shocking happened to me one day. Children see what adults cannot see. In one of my trips abroad, I was in a crowd, looking at a castle that someone built with sand. Suddenly I heard a commotion at my right. I looked in that direction and saw a small child struggling with the mother",Give some money; give some money..." The mother was asking him what he needed the money for. Finally, she succumbed and gave him a piece of money. This boy, ran toward me, and gave the money to —mien that huge crowd. This was in a place where I am not known. I took the money and laid my hands on that child and said, "Baby, you are blessed!"

Somehow, that child saw that I was not an ordinary man; a representative of the Most High God. He wanted to give something to God. He did not even have the money, but he collected it by force. I may not meet that child again, but I know he will prosper mightily.

Will you say to the Almighty God that, "My parents gave their best; I will give my all"? Will you say today", I will be greater than my parents?" Will you say", My seed will be greater than me? The choice is yours!

Prayer Points

1. Father, in every area possible, let me be far greater than my parents and let my children be far greater than I can ever be, in the name of Jesus.

2. Take a seed in your hands and pray thus, "Father, because of the offering I have in my hands, multiply me and my seeds far more greatly than me, in the name of Jesus."

3. Father, only you can bless me; bless me indeed, in the name of Jesus.

4. Father, give me a heart to give all that I have to you, in the name of Jesus.

5. Father, bless me with a blessing in its own class, in the name of Jesus.

6. Father, rebuke anything in me that refuses me from giving bountifully and sacrificially, in the name of Jesus.

7. Father, let every altar of selfishness and disobedience in me collapse, in the name of Jesus.

CHAPTER 11: MADE GREAT BY GRACE

I returned, and saw under the sun, that the race is not to the swift, nor the battle to the strong, neither yet bread to the wise, nor yet riches to men of understanding, nor yet favour to men of skill; but time and chance happeneth to them all. – Ecc. 9:11

The title of this chapter could as well have read "Made Rich by Grace."

When we talk about prosperity, it is in degrees.

The Poor – those who live in lack. In case you are still here, you will never be one of them again, in Jesus' name.

The Comfortable – before the secret is out, the next salary is paid.

The Rich – after they are done with their needs (eating and buying cloth, etc.), they still have some to put up as savings.

The Wealthy – they have enough for all their needs and they have a big chunk left in the bank as fixed deposit.

The Flourishing – these ones lend to nations. They have opulence. In the name of Jesus, you will get to this category!

Prosperity requires hard work. You have to be ready to work hard to prosper. Proverbs 22:29 says it all:

Seest thou a man diligent in his business? He shall stand before kings; he shall not stand before mean men.

However, one requires much more than hard work to succeed. 1 Samuel 2:9 reveals that no one prevails by strength.

He will keep the feet of his saints, and the wicked shall be silent in darkness; for by strength shall no man prevail.

It does not matter how hard you work; that does not determine how wealthy you become. The key text above reveals that the race is not to the swift neither is the battle to the strong. It is important, and we all know that we should sow seeds to prosper. Galatians 6:7 reiterates it:

Be not deceived; God is not mocked: for whatsoever a man soweth, that shall he also reap.

This means that when you sow nothing, you reap nothing. It is important also to sow bountifully. 2 Corinthians 9:6 says,

But this I say, He which soweth sparingly shall reap also sparingly; and he which soweth bountifully shall reap also bountifully.

When you sow bountifully, you reap bountifully. This can only happen when you sow on a good soil. Mathew 13:3-9 says:

And he spake many things unto them in parables, saying, Behold, a sower went forth to sow; And when he sowed, some seeds fell

by the way side, and the fowls came and devoured them up: Some fell upon stony places, where they had not much earth: and forthwith they sprung up, because they had no deepness of earth: And when the sun was up, they were scorched; and because they had no root, they withered away. And some fell among thorns; and the thorns sprung up, and choked them: But other fell into good ground, and brought forth fruit, some an hundredfold, some sixtyfold, some thirtyfold. Who hath ears to hear, let him hear.

The result of sowing is determined to a large extent by how good the soil is. This means that no matter how much you sow on a bad soil, stone, or rocky ground, you cannot get any harvest. Even if you get any harvest, it will be diminished.

However, when all is said and done, only God causes people to prosper. 1 Corinthians 3:6-7 states clearly;

I have planted, Apollos watered; but God gave the increase. So then neither is he that planteth any thing, neither he that watereth; but God that giveth the increase.

When you add this to the fact that God controls seasons, you will be convinced that truly, it is God who prospers.

Daniel answered and said, Blessed be the name of God for ever and ever: for wisdom and might are his: And he changeth the times and the seasons: he removeth kings, and setteth up kings: he giveth wisdom unto the wise, and knowledge to them that know understanding. – Daniel 2 : 20 - 21

God changes seasons; He decides what the season will be. If you sow the best of seeds in the best of soils, and rain refuses to fall, there will be a problem. Amos 4:7 says that God can choose to send the rain upon in one city and withhold it from another:

And also I have withholden the rain from you, when there were yet three months to the harvest: and I caused it to rain upon one city, and caused it not to rain upon another city: one piece was rained upon, and the piece whereupon it rained not withered.

God decides it all. He gives the increase. He decides when the rain will fall and where it will fall. I pray for you that from today, you will never labour in vain again, in the name of Jesus. That is why the Bible says in Proverbs 10:22 that

The blessing of the LORD, it maketh rich, and he addeth no sorrow with it.

If you read Genesis 14:1-14 you will see something spectacular:

And there was a famine in the land, beside the first famine that was in the days of Abraham. And Isaac went unto Abimelech king of the Philistines unto Gerar. And the LORD appeared unto him, and said, Go not down into Egypt; dwell in the land which I shall tell thee of: Sojourn in this land, and I will be with thee, and will bless thee; for unto thee, and unto thy seed, I will give all these countries, and I will perform the oath which I sware unto Abraham thy father; And I will make thy seed to multiply as the stars of heaven, and will give unto thy seed all these countries; and in thy seed shall all the nations of the earth be blessed; Because that Abraham obeyed my voice, and kept my

charge, my commandments, my statutes, and my laws. And Isaac dwelt in Gerar: And the men of the place asked him of his wife; and he said, She is my sister: for he feared to say, She is my wife; lest, said he, the men of the place should kill me for Rebekah; because she was fair to look upon. And it came to pass, when he had been there a long time, that Abimelech king of the Philistines looked out at a window, and saw, and, behold, Isaac was sporting with Rebekah his wife.

And Abimelech called Isaac, and said, Behold, of a surety she is thy wife: and how saidst thou, She is my sister? And Isaac said unto him, Because I said, Lest I die for her. And Abimelech said, What is this thou hast done unto us? one of the people might lightly have lien with thy wife, and thou shouldest have brought guiltiness upon us. And Abimelech charged all his people, saying, He that toucheth this man or his wife shall surely be put to death. Then Isaac sowed in that land, and received in the same year an hundredfold: and the LORD blessed him. And

the man waxed great, and went forward, and grew until he became very great: For he had possession of flocks, and possession of herds, and great store of servants: and the Philistines envied him.

There was famine in the land, but Isaac sowed in the same season and reaped a hundred fold. He kept prospering until the Philistines envied him. The question is; "Why would the Philistines envy him?" The answer is simple: He was not the only one sowing. They were also sowing, but he was the one prospering. Others were dying of famine and he was busy getting richer. God singled him out. The favour of God made him wealthy. The favour of God was so much that the whole nation envied him.

You do not know the meaning of prosperity until the nation begins to envy you– Until people begin to say, **"Are you the only one serving God? Are we not also serving Him"?** "We also pay our tithes and offerings; how come yours is as good as this"? when you get to that stage, when a whole nation begins to talk about you, then you know you have arrived. I prophesy upon you as you read this book that the favour of God will come upon you and nations will envy you, in the name of Jesus.

It is this understanding that it is not your effort alone that makes the difference that causes those who have wisdom to befriend God. That is why when it comes to worshiping God, they do it more than others. In 2 Samuel 6:12-17, David worshipped God with dancing; he danced so much that the whole nation noticed, including his wife. He was the king; he could have danced "majestically" (merely moving) like many Christians do. He could have applied kingly decorum, as a "big shot". But he danced so much in worship to God that his wife complained that it was too much. He recognised where God took him from. Remember where God picked you from, because you have a very rough idea of where He is taking you. If you are assured that you are heading to the top, shout **"Hallelujah!"**

And it was told king David, saying, The LORD hath blessed the house of Obededom, and all that pertaineth unto him, because of the ark of God. So David went and brought up the ark of God from the house of Obededom into the city of David with gladness. And it was so, that when they that bare the ark of the LORD had gone six paces, he sacrificed oxen and fatlings. And David danced before the LORD with all his might; and David was girded with a linen ephod. So David and all the house of Israel brought up the ark of the LORD with shouting, and with the sound of the trumpet. And as the ark of the LORD came into the city of David, Michal Saul's daughter looked through a window, and saw king David leaping and dancing before the LORD; and she despised him in her heart. And they brought in the ark of the LORD, and set it in his place, in the midst of the tabernacle that David had pitched for it: and David offered burnt offerings and peace offerings before the LORD. –2 Samuel 6:12-17

Those who realise that it takes God to prosper worship Him exuberantly; they worship God lavishly. In 2 Chronicles 1:6-15, Solomon came to offer a thousand offerings. He knew no one had ever done that before. The priests were astonished. He kept going until a thousand bullocks were offered. None of them knew why he worshipped God so lavishly. Solomon looked at the background of his father and mother. He realised that they had met in adultery before his birth. How can a child of these two people become king? He was not even qualified to be made a king above his elder brothers. But God favoured him.

If you look at the history of your mother and father, and your history before you met Christ, God has still remained too generous to you. If you do nothing but just sing and praise him for the whole day and night, it is not yet enough. When you see people worshiping God lavishly and exuberantly; spending money for God as if they are mad; they know what they are doing. Nobody is going to get to the level of lending to nations by treating God as a junior partner.

Prosperity is by grace and grace alone. It is God who will look down and say, "I will make this fellow great!" You have to learn to partner with God in a big way.

Many years ago when the highest denomination of the naira was twenty naira, God spoke to me one day and sa"idW, hat type of pastor do you want to be?" Being a mathematician, I do not answer a question until I understand it. So I aske"dW, hat do you mean, Lord?"

He replied, "Do you want to be the best or worst; do you want to be the richest or poorest"? So, I answered affirmatively:" I want to be the best and riche"stO.ne day when offerings were collected in service, the Lord said to m"eW, hat about giving the highest denomination as offering"? I answered, "Yes Lord"! So I began to give twenty naira. It was a lot of money. At another service the Lord said, "What about doubling the amount of offering?" My "Yes Lord" became lower in volume. But I doubled my offering.

After a short while he said again to me during an offering collection, "What about tripling the amount?" I could barely respond to Him. But I obeyed.

After a short while, the Lord responded with harvest. Every day, someone would come and give me money for personal use. It never failed; whether I needed money or not, someone would give me money daily. It was so much that one day when I went to Benin to minister at the Full Gospel Business Men's Fellowship; I knelt down beside the bed to pray after ministration. After thanking God for all the souls won and mighty things he did that night, I told him, "Daddy, nobody gave me money today. I don't know why. Maybe you should add it to the next day and pay doub"le .Before I could lie on the bed, at midnight, someone knocked on the door of my room. When I opened, he said", The Lord said I should give you this money. I didn't want to give you, but I couldn't sleep. Here it is." That was wonderful. What a faithful God we serve!

I am talking to you about what is happening in my life, and not theory. As far as I am concerned, all the honours have nothing to do to me, unless it has to do about God. Some years ago when the Nigerian Government wanted to honour a hundred people, they chose only one pastor to be on the list. That pastor was me. I then remembered God's question many years ago; **"What kind of Pastor do you want to be?" In the same vein, I ask you,**

"What kind of child of God do you want to –be the least or the greatest; the worst or the best; the poorest of the richest?"

We are made great by grace; we are made wealthy by grace. But firstly, we are saved by grace. Receive the grace of God that gives unlimited greatness now, in the mighty name of Jesus.

Prayer Points

1. Give God a great shout of Hallelujah!

2. Father, because you control seasons and times, let my season of tremendous overflow in every area of life begin right now, in the name of Jesus.

3. Father, let my season of unlimited greatness begin right now, in the name of Jesus.

4. Father, I want to be the best; I want to be the greatest; I want to be the richest in my generation; so let it be, Daddy, in the name Jesus.

5. Father, bless me so mightily that I will lend to nations, in the name of Jesus.

6. Father, make me flourish so mightily, in the name of Jesus.

7. Father, help me to get to the top, in the name of Jesus.

8. Father, let today mark a new beginning for me, in the name of Jesus

9. Father, I ask for grace today to serve you more than anyone else in my generation, in the name of Jesus.

10. Father, make me a special gift to my generation all the days of my life, in the name of Jesus.

CHAPTER 12: YOUR PROSPERITY IS SETTLED

The young lions do lack, and suffer hunger: but they that seek the LORD shall not want any good thing. – Psalm 34:10

Your prosperity is by divine decree. The first divine decree of your prosperity is found in the Bible text above. The Word of God here does not say, "…those who seek the Lord may not.".. He says they "shall not lack any good thing." This verse is written in the language of a decree with God's seal on it. The only way you can lack any good thing" is when good thing comes and you personally reject it.

The second decree is in Deuteronomy 28:11:

And the LORD shall make thee plenteous in goods, in the fruit of thy body, and in the fruit of thy cattle, and in the fruit of thy ground, in

the land which the LORD sware unto thy fathers to give thee.

The text above records that the Lord shall make you plenteous in goods. It does not say plenteous in spirit. What are goods? They are cars, houses, cloths, land, and anything money can buy - material things!

Further, this text talks about the fruit of your body. This means you will have children, as many as you want. You will also have lots of money to take care of them. If you have any domestic animal, goat, sheep, poultry, cattle, et–c . God says they will keep on prospering. If you plant anything, it will come out very well. Now examine the next verse carefully.

The LORD shall open unto thee his good treasure, the heaven to give the rain unto thy land in his season, and to bless all the work of thine hand: and thou shalt lend unto many nations, and thou shalt not borrow. – Deuteronomy 28:11

God is not talking about you lending money to individuals, but to nations. He added one thing;"...and thou shalt not borrow". This is talking about wealth that is very difficult for human beings to imagine.

One of the reasons many are poor today is because they take God too lightly. Concerning salvation, they believe the blood of Jesus cleanses from all sins. On divine healing, they claim, "by His stripes we are healed". Talking about the kind of wealth that will enable them to lend to nations, doubts are raised. They will ask questions like: "How can people become that rich? Are there people like that in this world?"

In addition, another divine decree exists in Deuteronomy 28:13:

And the LORD shall make thee the head, and not the tail; and thou shalt be above only, and thou shalt not be beneath; if that thou hearken unto the commandments of the LORD thy God, which I command thee this day, to observe and to do them.

We have earlier observed that the poor are servants to the rich. Have you ever experienced being sacked at work?– You left home in the morning rejoicing that you were going to work, and on getting to workplace, they said you have a letter. When you opened the letter, you read: "...We regret to let you know that your services are no longer required in this organization..."You came to work with joy, but left with sorrow. So how can you explain that the poor is not a slave to the rich? God in his awesomeness is telling you in the text above, "That is not my plan for you! My plan for you is to be a director yourself."

You may ask, **"If we all become directors, who will then be the servants?"** – The unbelievers of course! That is their lot. We are children of the Most High. We are princes and princesses of the King of kings.

Let us examine another decree of prosperity in Psalm 37:18:

The LORD knoweth the days of the upright: and their inheritance shall be for ever.

There will be a time of prosperity. There will also be time of austerity. There will be the time of plenty. There will also be the time for famine. As far as God's children are concerned, even in the time of famine, they shall be satisfied.

I remember a story I heard about a man. He was strolling in London and saw a car factory, which happened to be where they manufactured a brand of the car he rides. He said, "What? Is this where they manufactured my car? Why can't they put the place right?"

The following day, he came to the factory and said", I want to buy this factory." One of the company officials replied, "Where will you get the money to buy it? It is not only cars we manufacture, but aircraft too." The man said, "I want you to tell me how much it is." They thought he was joking, or probably out of his mind. The official told him the cost of the factory. There and then, he wrote a cheque to cover the amount even with interest, and the factory became his.

When we go to some television stations and say we want to preach Jesus Christ, they say. "No! This is network channel; we don't allow this here." We should be able to say, "How much is this television studio? Just tell me how much and we will give you double the price." This is why we are asking for prosperity. We are not asking for prosperity in order to be able to marry two wives. God forbid! We need money in order to be able to accomplish the work of God assigned to us. If we do not take over this country, those who are holding money will take over this country from us. This is why you must be prosperous.

How will God do it? Psalm 113:7 explains it:

He raiseth up the poor out of the dust, and lifteth the needy out of the dunghill;

The Bible says that the poor lives in the dunghill. Compared to where you can be, you are living in a dunghill. The Almighty God will reach down and pick you up by the hand, that is, if you raise your hand to him. If you raise your hand and say, "I need help!" He will lift you up in Jesus' name. It will not be God's fault if He reaches down with His hand and you fold your hands.

No one is completely comfortable until he can do whatever he wants to do when he wants to do it. Let me put it in another way. Anybody who cannot do what he wants to do when he wants to do it is a prisoner. A prisoner cannot go where he wants to go; cannot eat what he wants to eat. God will reach down and grab those who are ready and lift them up with His supernatural power.

A little imagination on how God will work these things out leaves us in awe. Look at 1 Chronicles 29:11-12:

Thine, O LORD, is the greatness, and the power, and the glory, and the victory, and the majesty: for all that is in the heaven and in the earth is thine; thine is the kingdom, O LORD, and thou art exalted as head above all. Both riches and honour come of thee, and thou reignest over all; and in thine hand ispower and might; and in thine hand it is to make great, and to give strength unto all.

The Bible says here that God, our Father owns it all; everything. Not only does He have everything; the power to distribute it as He wishes is with Him too. If He has power to share like this, what is He going to do? This could be found in Psalm 68:10:

Thy congregation hath dwelt therein: thou, O God, hast prepared of thy goodness for the poor.

Out of His goodness and the wealth He has, God has divided them into portions, and the poor have theirs. The question"Wish; at about those already taken by the unbelievers?" The devil knows that most

Christians feel that they do not need money, and as such, those who serve him can have the money. He knows that money is there. He knows they belong to God, but if the sons of God say they do not want it, the slaves can have it.

What will God do to the wealth the slaves already have if His children rise and say they want it back? Isaiah 61:5-6 says,

And strangers shall stand and feed your flocks, and the sons of the alien shall be your plowmen and your vinedressers. But ye shall be named the Priests of the LORD: men shall call you the Ministers of our God: ye shall eat the riches of the Gentiles, and in their glory shall ye boast yourselves.

As discussed above, those who are not of God will be messengers if all Christians become directors. We will put them to work and sweat, and after sweating, we will collect the gain and give them a little to sustain them. They will be satisfied with it, just as Christians are satisfied when strangers are feeding them. Those who are not supposed to be in authority and control of wealth are there because they grabbed your Father's money. Then they make Christians labour and sweat 24 hours a day. Before 5.am, you wake up, not because you want to pray, but because you do not want to miss the bus to work. Moreover, if you get late to work, the one you call a slave will issue you a query. If you say you are a son of God, what type of son are you? You have to take your position now!

In the above text, the Lord promises that if you walk according to His commands, you shall be named the priest of the Lord. Men shall call you the ministers of our God. You will eat the riches of the Gentiles, and you shall boast yourself in the glory of the Gentiles. Take what belongs to you. If God is your Father, then what your Father has is yours.

Prayer Points

1. Father, settle me financially, in the name of Jesus.

2. Father, pour your grace of unlimited financial breakthrough upon me, in the name of Jesus.

3. Father, my life is available for the transfer of the wealth of the Gentiles into my life, in the name of Jesus.

4. Father, remove every fear in me that is limiting me from financial exploits, in the name of Jesus.

5. Everlasting Father, saturate my life with your blessings, in the name of Jesus.

6. Father, clothe me with the gab of obedience, in the name of Jesus.

7. Father, position me to take up my rightful position as your son in global financial matters, in the name of Jesus.

CHAPTER 13: DELIVERANCE FROM POVERTY

Arise, shine; for thy light is come, and the glory of the LORD is risen upon thee. For, behold, the darkness shall cover the earth, and gross darkness the people: but the LORD shall arise upon thee, and his glory shall be seen upon thee. And the Gentiles shall come to thy light, and kings to the brightness of thy rising. Lift up thine eyes round about, and see: all they gather themselves together, they come to thee: thy sons shall come from far, and thy daughters shall be nursed at thy side. Then thou shalt see, and flow together, and thine heart shall fear, and be enlarged; because the abundance of the sea shall be converted unto thee, the forces of the Gentiles shall come unto thee. The multitude of camels shall cover thee, the dromedaries of Midian and Ephah; all they from Sheba shall come: they shall bring gold and incense; and they shall shew forth the praises of the LORD. All the flocks of Kedar shall be gathered together unto thee, the rams of Nebaioth shall minister unto thee: they shall come up with acceptance on mine altar, and I will glorify the house of my glory. – Isaiah 60:1-7

Poverty is a curse; it is an evil that destroys. It is important we break the curse of poverty. Some people struggle so hard and get nothing. The reason is that somebody somewhere has put a curse upon them. What are the signs that a curse is working upon your finances, and how can you get rid of the curses? There are five major ways to recognise this.

1. Working Like an Elephant and Eating Like an Ant– if your gain comes through very great hardship and sorrows, there might be a curse working against you. In other words, if you have to sweat so much before you can get a little to eat, all along the way, there is one sorrow or one problem or another. It means there is a curse working somewhere. In Genesis 3:17-19, there was a curse pronounced on Adam:

And unto Adam he said, Because thou hast hearkened unto the voice of thy wife, and hast eaten of the tree, of which I commanded thee, saying, Thou shalt not eat of it: cursed is the ground for thy sake; in sorrow shalt thou eat of it all the days of thy life; Thorns also and thistles shall it bring forth to thee; and thou shalt eat the herb of the field; In the sweat of thy face shalt thou eat bread, till thou return unto the ground; for out of it wast thou taken: for dust thou art, and unto dust shalt thou return.

Here, we have the first curse placed on man. God sai"dY, ou will sweat before you eat". Does that suggest that he was not working before? No! God asked him to dress the garden and have control of it, and eat whatever he wanted. The point is that the work he was doing before the curse was easy. He would do a little and will harvest a lot; a little effort and plenty gain.

After the curse, the reverse was to be the case. He would work like an elephant and eat like an ant. Other people will trade with the same capital that you are trading with. They will make one trip, buy the goods they want, and as soon as they arrive, customers are waiting for them. They sell all to customers, make their gain, go home, and rest for some days. They go again and buy, and as they return, those who are going to buy are waiting again. You saw them prosper and thought it was the best business. Then you gathered some money, made the same trip, brought your own merchandise and nobody is interested. There is a curse working!

If you are a true child of God, what God says in Proverbs 10:22 should be happening.

The blessing of the LORD, it maketh rich, and he addeth no sorrow with it. – Proverbs 10:22

In other words, as far as God is concerned, you can become rich without sorrow. You do not have to work until you die before you become wealthy. When you begin to work so hard and you are getting so little, something must be wrong somewhere.

2. Unsuccessful Ventures – When you find someone going from one business to another without succeeding in one, they become commercial vagabonds. There must be something wrong somewhere. If whatever you try fails, whereas other people are doing the same business and are succeeding, definitely, a curse must be working somewhere.

In Genesis 4:9-12, there was a curse again that God placed on a certain man:

And the LORD said unto Cain, Where is Abel thy brother? And he said, I know not: Am I my brother's keeper? And he said, What hast thou done? the voice of thy brother's blood crieth unto me from the ground. And now art thou cursed from the earth, which hath opened her mouth to receive thy brother's blood from thy hand; When thou tillest the ground, it shall not henceforth yield unto thee her strength; a fugitive and a vagabond shalt thou be in the earth.

When somebody becomes a commercial vagabond, there is a curse working somewhere because the promise of God for those who are doing His will is this:

And it shall come to pass, if thou shalt hearken diligently unto the voice of the LORD thy God, to observe and to do all his commandments

which I command thee this day, that the LORD thy God will set thee on high above all nations of the earth: And all these blessings shall come on thee, and overtake thee, if thou shalt hearken unto the voice of the LORD thy God. – Deuteronomy 28:1-2

God did not say that you will be running after blessings; the blessings should be running after you. They will overtake you. Wherever you go, blessings will come upon you mightily. Even when you say they are too much and you run away from there, by the time you arrive in the town where you are going, other blessings will be waiting for you there. Instead of becoming a commercial vagabond, wherever you are, if there is no curse, the Bible says that blessings will be overtaking you.

There was a certain man who was not promoted in his office for seven years. Someone stole his file and hid it. Anytime they wanted to discuss promotion matters, the people to recommend him never found his file. Then he came to us, and we asked him to give his life to Jesus Christ. He did. the following month, there was change in the leadership of his department, and the new man asked for the files of everyone in his department. They looked for this man's file and could not find it. The new Head of Department ordered them to find it. Finally, they found the file. They discovered that there was no recommendation for promotion for seven years in this man's file. The new boss then gave the man double promotion just to compensate for all the years that had been lost.

3. Sudden and Rapid Decline– the third way to know if a curse is at work is when there is sudden and rapid deterioration in productivity. If your productivity suddenly goes down and it is very rapid, then there must be a curse working. You may feel it is because things are hard in the country.

Whenever there is a curse placed upon a business or a particular fellow, rapid changes will begin to happen, and it would move fast. Within a year, someone who is already on top can become someone who is beneath. For example, I know of someone who used to have forty vehicles for his business. Within one year, there was only one left.

Now in the morning as he returned into the city, he hungered. And when he saw a fig tree in the way, he came to it, and found nothing thereon, but leaves only, and said unto it, Let no fruit grow on thee henceforward forever. And presently the fig tree withered away. And when the disciples saw it, they marvelled, saying, How soon is the fig tree withered away! – Matthew 21:18-20

A curse was placed on the fig tree. Another Bible text says by the time they returned the following day, not only had it dried up, it had been uprooted. A curse can reduce what has been producing fruits to a dry tree overnight. Concerning those who are doing His will, upon whom there is no curse, what the God says in Psalm 1:3 applies.

And he shall be like a tree planted by the rivers of water, that bringeth forth his fruit in his season; his leaf also shall not wither; and whatsoever he doeth shall prosper. –Psalm 1:3

If it happens that a sudden calamity has gripped your business, or you are suddenly purged in your placed of work without any fault of yours; instead of making progress, you find yourself seriously retrogressing; it does not matter whatever reason you think; a curse is working.

4. Abortive Efforts – the fourth way to recognize if a curse is working on an individual or a business is through abortive efforts. When one is about arriving, but never arrives. You follow up a contract, but it fell off your grip; or even if you get the contract and are asked to come for the mobilization fee, you get there and they say, "Sorry sir. The Managing Director has travelled. When he comes you can have the mon"eyH.e travelled, and never came back.

In this case, something must be working underneath. Many times, the way is open and when you are about to go in, suddenly, the door is shut. Again, another door will open, and when you want to go in, the door is shut against you. Many a time, you even spend a lot of money to get to where you are about to reach. Just before it is handed over to you, the door is shut. It is because a curse is working against you.

This is the type of curse that worked against Jericho. They had plenty of water. Their land was very plain and very beautiful. Their wives got pregnant, but they never put to bed. Their goats and sheep got pregnant, but the pregnancies were aborted. It was because a curse was placed on that city by Joshua (Joshua 6:26). 2 Kings 2:19 say it all:

And the men of the city said unto Elisha, Behold, I pray thee, the situation of this city is pleasant, as my lord seeth: but the water is naught, and the ground barren.

5. Inability to Account for Income – another way to know if a curse is at work is the inability to account for your income; it keeps disappearing. The money comes quite alright; you collect it, even count it, but how does it disappear? You can never tell what is happening. If you are to sit and calculate the money that has come into your hands for the past three years, you will be amazed how many thousands or millions of naira it would be. It will be difficult to point at one thing or an achievement done with the money. When such things happen, there is a curse at work.

In Haggai 1:6, God says

Ye have sown much, and bring in little; ye eat, but ye have not enough; ye drink, but ye are not filled with drink; ye clothe you, but there is none warm; and he that earneth

wages earneth wages to put it into a bag with holes.

Verse 9 of the same chapter says something similar:

Ye looked for much, and, lo, it cameto little; and when ye brought it home, I did blow upon it. Why? saith the LORD of hosts. Because of mine house that is waste, and ye run every man unto his own house.

God is trying to tell us that there are two ways which you can discover that the money is coming in, but you do not know what is happening to it. It might have gone into a bag with holes. The money may be coming in, but is going out as fast as it is coming in.

Many people have this experience. They are collecting money, and they may say, "I am setting this portion aside to build a house." Just when the money is enough to begin the building, somebody very precious to them may fall sick in the family. They will spend all the savings in the hospital. They will begin to save again, and then something will happen again in the family. Someone may be arrested for a crime he did not commit, and the savings will be spent to resolve the case.

If you fit into these five categories, you sincerely need deliverance. If the curse placed upon you is from a man or Satan, it is easy to settle. We will just break the curse in the name of Jesus! Not only shall it be broken, but it will become impossible for them to curse you again. He that has the authority to bless does not sweat before destroying curses.

A curse can also come from God directly. There is only one way to get out of it. I remember a clear case of someone who has been going from one business to another. He tried all cases in different direction and failed in all. So I got concerned and said, "Lord, please I want to remove the curse placed on this ma"n.God said to me, "Sorry son, you cannot remove it because I am the one who placed it there."

To remove a curse placed by God, firstly you must repent. Haggai 1:5 says, "Now therefore thus saith the LORD of hosts; Consider your ways." In verse 7, it says again,

"Thus saith the LORD of hosts; Consider your ways."

I am now saying to you",Consider your ways, and examine your lifestyle." Find out where you have gone wrong. Ask yourself questions and give honest answers to them. After you might have considered your ways and found out where you got off the track, then do what God says.

The second way to escape God's curses is to return your tithes.

Will a man rob God? Yet ye have robbed me. But ye say, Wherein have we robbed thee? In tithes and offerings. Ye are cursed with a curse: for ye have robbed me, even this whole nation. Bring ye all the tithes into the storehouse, that there may be meat in mine house, and prove me now herewith, saith the LORD of hosts, if I will not open you the windows of heaven, and pour you out a blessing, that there shall not be room enough to receive it. And I will rebuke the devourer for your sakes, and he shall not destroy the fruits of your ground; neither shall your vine cast her fruit before the time in the field, saith the LORD of hosts. And all nations shall call you blessed: for ye shall be a delightsome land, saith the LORD of hosts. – Malachi 3:8-12

God is saying that whatever you stole should be restored. In other words, those things biting your money - the abortive efforts - will stop. All the nations of the earth will call you blessed. You will become the envy of the world. You will become so wealthy that nations shall become envious of you. If you obey God's commands, He will surprise you.

Joel 2:12 says,

Therefore also now, saith the LORD, turn ye even to me with all your heart, and with fasting, and with weeping, and with mourning:

In the 25th verse through the 27th verse, God says:

Fear not, O land; be glad and rejoice: for the LORD will do great things. Be not afraid, ye beasts of the field: for the pastures of the wilderness do spring, for the tree beareth her fruit, the fig tree and the vine do yield their strength. Be glad then, ye children of Zion, and rejoice in the LORD your God: for he hath given you the former rain moderately, and he will cause to come down for you the rain, the former rain, and the latter rain in the first month. And the floors shall be full of wheat, and the fats shall overflow with wine and oil. And I will restore to you the years that the locust hath eaten, the cankerworm, and the caterpiller, and the palmerworm, my great army which I sent among you. And ye shall eat in plenty, and be satisfied, and praise the name of the LORD your God, that hath dealt

wondrously with you: and my people shall never be ashamed. And ye shall know that I am in the midst of Israel, and that I am the LORD your God, and none else: and my people shall never be ashamed.

When God says He wants to do great things, those things must be embarrassingly great. In fact, what God will call great is what you will call impossible. It takes only one a miracle from God to lift you from the dust and put you on the throne. When God is going to do it, you will not know when it is going to happen.

When God starts blessing you, the first sign to notice is that you would not have finished a month's salary (if you are a salary earner) before the next one rolls in. This was the first miracle that started in my life when I began to pay my tithe.

Before I began to pay my tithe, I had a car and a driver. I paid the driver about twenty naira as monthly salary. By the middle of the month, I would borrow money from my driver to put petrol in my car. So when they began to talk about tithe, I said", Nonsense! 100 percent is not even enough to put petrol in my car, and now they are asking me to make do with 90 percent of my salary."

However, in the first month that I paid my tithe, I did not borrow money from my driver. What remained at the end of the month was not much, but something remained. The new month met something of the old in my pocket. That was the beginning of the end of the curse on my finances.

The curse in your life will come to an end if you will repent and do everything that the Lord asks you to do. What you have stolen from God, I appeal to you, restore, and he will surprise you. Within one day, He will do what nobody can do for you in a thousand years.

From hence forth, you shall no more be a burden to people. God will make you a blessing to your generation, in the name of Jesus. Joseph became a channel of blessing to his generation. God repositioned him within a twinkling of an eye from the lowest ebb to the exalted position of a prime minister.

For you to fulfil the divine mandate of being born for a blessing, you must be saturated with the spirit of prayer. It is when you pray that the power of God will cut off every limiting fetter to your breakthroughs, success, family life, marriage, prosperity, healing and deliverance. God wants to give you a holistic visitation.

Prayer Points

1. Father, I claim my redemption against poverty, in the name of Jesus.

2. Father, I possess the key of prosperity, in the name of Jesus.

3. Father, I possess abundance upon my family, in the name of Jesus.

4. Father, release favour upon my works, in the name of Jesus.

5. Father, break the barrier of poverty in my life, in the name of Jesus.

6. Sorrow of poverty, leave my life alone, in the name of Jesus!

7. Father, deliver me from the shame of poverty, in Jesus' name.

CHAPTER 14: HELP IS ON THE WAY

And the word of the LORD came unto him, saying, Arise, get thee to Zarephath, which belongeth to Zidon, and dwell there: behold, I have commanded a widow woman there to sustain thee. So he arose and went to Zarephath. And when he came to the gate of the city, behold, the widow woman was there gathering of sticks: and he called to her, and said, Fetch me, I pray thee, a little water in a vessel, that I may drink. And as she was going to fetch it, he called to her, and said, Bring me, I pray thee, a morsel of bread in thine hand. And she said, As the LORD thy God liveth, I have not a cake, but an handful of meal in a barrel, and a little oil in a cruse: and, behold, I am gathering two sticks, that I may go in and dress it for me and my son, that we may eat it, and die. And Elijah said unto her, Fear not; go and do as thou hast said: but make me thereof a little cake first, and bring it unto me, and after make for thee and for thy son. For thus saith the LORD God of Israel, The barrel of meal shall not waste, neither shall the cruse of oil fail, until the day that the LORD sendeth rain upon the earth. And she went and did according to the saying of Elijah: and she, and he, and her house, did eat many days. And the barrel of meal wasted not, neither did the cruse of oil fail, according to the word of the LORD, which he spake by Elijah. – 1 Kings 17:8-16

I believe that the help you are expecting from the Almighty God will arrive today, in the name of Jesus. This is a story of a widow. A widow is someone who used to know joy; someone who always remembers the day of her wedding. This particular widow has a son. So she could also remember the day she had a baby boy. But things had turned against her. Her husband had died, and financially, everything turned upside down. From this story, it is clear that whatever job she was doing had been lost. Whatever savings she had was finished. Little by little, everything she had dwindled until there was only one meal left.

So this widow sat and took a decision. Rather than sit down and watch her son die, she decided to prepare the last meal, eat it with her son, and they would commit suicide. Note that she did not say they would wait for death after the last meal. She said they would eat the last meal and die. That means suicide— finish the meal and end it all. So she went out to collect two sticks. You can imagine her situation that day. The agony of her life was too much; little wonder she was determined to end it all. She was not even a Jew or the people of God. So suicide meant nothing much.

However, unknown to her, help was on the way. The Almighty God already held a conference about her that instead of her to die, she would live; instead of her to die in poverty, she would live to know the meaning of abundance. You may be in a desperate situation, but I have come to announce to you that help is on the way!

Suddenly, a prophet arrived and asked for water. She gave him water despite the fact that there had been no rain. Water was scarce.

She shared the little she had with the prophet with the thought that she would not need water again after that day because she wanted to end it all. As she went to fetch the water, Elijah asked for bread also. In the widow's reply to the prophet as seen in the key text above, we will learn a few deep things.

To Whom Will God Send Help?

1. He Who Knows That God is Alive – "...And she said, As the LORD thy God liveth, I have not a cake..." She was saying that although she did not know much about the God of Elijah, she knows that He is alive. So the question I want to ask you is, "From whom will your help come? Knowing that God is alive will encourage you to know that he hears prayers. Dead gods do not hear prayers. There is nothing anyone can do to convince you to the contrary. Our God is alive! Our Redeemer lives! This has nothing to do with your present situation.

Psalm 65:2 says this about God; "O thou that hearest prayer, unto thee shall all flesh come". Because God is alive, He hears prayers. Not only does He hear prayers, He also sees all that is going on. 2 Chronicles 16:9 says,

"For the eyes of the LORD run to and fro throughout the whole earth, to shew himself strong on the behalf of them whose heart is perfect toward him. Herein thou hast done

foolishly: therefore from henceforth thou shalt have wars."

God sees it all, no matter what you are going through. Whatever is happening to you, God sees it all. Psalm 46:1 says that, "God is our refuge and strength, a very present help in trouble." He hears prayers. He sees, and is always ready to help.

2. Someone Who Believes in God– If you do not believe that God is alive, you cannot believe what God's prophet tells you. Elijah replied the widow in the name of the God who is alive; who the widow already believes in.

2 Chronicles 20:20 says,

"And they rose early in the morning, and went forth into the wilderness of Tekoa: and as they went forth, Jehoshaphat stood and said, Hear me, O Judah, and ye inhabitants of Jerusalem; Believe in the LORD your God, so shall ye be established; believe his prophets, so shall ye prosper."

The one who will receive help is the one who not only believes in God, but also believes in God's prophet. If you have faith in God, all things are possible (Mark 9:23).

In 1983, we held the first convention in the Redeemed Camp at Mowe, Ogun State. That area was the headquarters of armed robbery and all sorts of nefarious activities. I heard God clearly concerning holding the convention there that year. We had to construct a camp in three months. Resources were limited. I thank God I was not voted out as General Overseer that year. The whole idea sounded crazy.

To make matters worse, we dug countless wells and they were collapsing. This was because the ground on the camp site is muddy. This continued until we had a week to the convention. The level of complaints increased greatly. Some leaders were already suggesting we quickly move back to the old site, which was congested for that year's convention. But I trusted my God and He proved to me that He is alive.

With one week left before the convention, something happened. On a Saturday, a man was passing by and drove in to see what we were doing. He asked us what was going on, and we told him we were constructing a camp site for our church. So he asked us what our greatest need was. I told him we needed water, since all the wells we dug collapsed. He exclaimed, "You don't need a well here; what you need is a borehole". I responded by saying", We know; but where is the money for that now?" The man brought in his engineers and started digging water for us for free. Just two days before the convention, they struck water. We already started constructing the overhead tank for the borehole even when they were yet to strike water. On the eve of the convention, we linked the borehole to the overhead tank! It was a helpless situation, but God sent help to me. In your critical moment, may God send help to you, in the mighty name of Jesus!

3. One who is willing to Surrender All to God –

When the widow agreed to give all she had to the prophet, she surrendered all. She was ready to die with her son after their last meal. Now it appears they will not be having any last meal before their death. She surrendered all. She was willing to put God first. If you will receive God's help you must show Him that He is the number one in your life.

Romans 12:1 says,

I beseech you therefore, brethren, by the mercies of God, that ye present your bodies a living sacrifice, holy, acceptable unto God, which is your reasonable service.

Anyone who will receive help from God must be willing to put down his life on the altar of God. When we read Proverbs 3:9-10, we are to give first fruits to honour God. It is not because God is hungry. Honour God and leave the rest to Him.

When we talk about putting God first, surrendering all to God, we must take it seriously. Years ago when I became the General Overseer of our Church, the income of the church was very small. By the time the pastors are paid, there was little or nothing left. I had just resigned as the Acting Head of Department of Mathematics at University of Ilorin. I was thinking about how to survive. So I applied for my gratuity, and to God's glory, it came. I was paid a huge sum of money. I was happy that at least I could survive until the finances of the church increases.

Then I suddenly remembered that I was under God's government. So I asked the Lord what to do with my gratuity. So many Christians do not hear God when it comes to giving. They only hear God when it comes to receiving. The Lord replied me immediately, "Divide the gratuity into three". I was happy. Then He said, "Give one part to so and so ministry said", Yes Lord". Of the remaining two portions, I thought it would be to save some, and put the other in fixed deposit; or even invest. God demanded that the remaining two portions be also given to two other ministries. This was so tough. But I did as he commanded. Then He said something to me: "I will be your Source!"

Ever since then, the Lord has never failed me. He has always remained faithful to His promise to me. If you want help from the Lord, believe that God is alive; believe in God and his prophet; believe it when God speaks to you, and lay everything on the altar. He will then prove to you that He is the ever present help in trouble.

Prayer Points

1. Father, you are the help of the helpless; help Lord, in the name of Jesus.

2. Father, I need your help; help me by your mercy, in the name of Jesus.

3. Father, help me speedily, in the name of Jesus.

4. Help of the Helpless, help me, in the name of Jesus.

5. Father, even today, may help come my way, in the name of Jesus.

6. Father, in every facet of my life, do not let me lack again, in the name of Jesus.

CHAPTER 15: THE BLESSED OF THE LORD

The blessing of the LORD, it maketh rich, and he addeth no sorrow with it. – Prov. 10:22

The above passage of the Bible is simple to understand. It tells us that there could be wealth with sorrows. In 2 Kings 5:1, the Bible says that Naaman was a very wealthy man, but had an incurable disease. So it is possible to be rich and be sick. There are some sicknesses and diseases that money cannot cure. There are a lot of rich people that doctors have told there is nothing more to help them with.

In Ecclesiastes 5:11, the Bible says,

The sleep of a labouring man is sweet, whether he eat little or much: but the abundance of the rich will not suffer him to sleep.

It is possible to be rich and not be able to sleep. The abundance of the rich can deny them sleep. So money can buy a very expensive bed, but cannot buy sleep.

According to 2 Kings 4:8-17,

And it fell on a day, that Elisha passed to Shunem, where was a great woman; and she constrained him to eat bread. And so it was, that as oft as he passed by, he turned in thither to eat bread. And she said unto her husband, Behold now, I perceive that this isan holy man of God, which passeth by us continually. Let us make a little chamber, I pray thee, on the wall; and let us set for him there a bed, and a table, and a stool, and a candlestick: and it shall be, when he cometh to us, that he shall turn in thither. And it fell on a day, that he came thither, and he turned into the chamber, and lay there. And he said to Gehazi his servant, Call this Shunammite. And when he had called her, she stood before him. And he said unto him, Say now unto her, Behold, thou hast been careful for us with all this care; what is to be done for thee?

wouldest thou be spoken for to the king, or to the captain of the host? And she answered, I dwell among mine own people. And he said, What then is to be done for her? And Gehazi answered, Verily she hath no child, and her husband is old. And he said, Call her. And when he had called her, she stood in the door. And he said, About this season, according to the time of life, thou shalt embrace a son. And she said, Nay, my lord, thou man of God, do not lie unto thine handmaid. And the woman conceived, and bare a son at that season that Elisha had said unto her, according to the time of life.

The Shunammite woman was a great and wealthy woman. She was so wealthy that she could build any house she wanted. But she was barren. It is possible to be rich and have a very important need that is left unmet. It is possible to be rich and sick. It is possible to be rich and have insomnia (an inability to sleep; chronic sleeplessness). It is even possible to be rich and not be able to eat. I pray for you that the type of wealth that will not allow you to sleep will not come to you, in the name of Jesus. If there is a desire in your heart for so long, may the Almighty God fulfil it today, in the name of Jesus.

Above all, it is possible to be rich and not have any sorrow. Ecclesiastes 5:19 says,

Every man also to whom God hath given riches and wealth, and hath given him power to eat thereof, and to take his portion, and to rejoice in his labour; this is the gift of God.

God can bless you in such a way that you are rich and you are able to eat of the things that you have. You have wealth and you are able to enjoy it. I know what that passage is saying. I had a friend who was so rich that when he died, in one of his bank accounts in far away Australia, he had $256,000,000 (two hundred and fifty six million dollars). This did not include money in many other continents – England, USA, etc. On one occasion, he forgot that he deposited £8,000,000 (eight million pounds) in the bank. But sadly, the only food this man could eat is milk. He could only drink milk. I do not presently have such an amount of wealth, but I can eat any delicacy I want. Am I not blessed? Definitely, I am.

Genesis 29:34-35 tells us of how wealthy Abraham was:

And he said, I am Abraham's servant. And the LORD hath blessed my master greatly; and he is become great: and he hath given him flocks, and herds, and silver, and gold, and menservants, and maidservants, and camels, and asses.

Abraham was very rich and was without sickness. He was strong enough to produce a child at hundred. That is the kind of the blessing the Almighty God will give you.

In Genesis 21:1-6, in the house of Abraham, there was laughter continually. It was a house full of laughter. In the name of Jesus, not only will your house be wealthy, but it will be full of laughter.

Malachi 3:10-11 says,

Bring ye all the tithes into the storehouse, that there may be meat in mine house, and prove me now herewith, saith the LORD of hosts, if I will not open you the windows of heaven, and pour you out a blessing, that there shall not be room enough to receive it. And I will rebuke the devourer for your sakes, and he shall not destroy the fruits of your ground; neither shall your vine cast her fruit before the time in the field, saith the LORD of hosts.

Here the Bible says that when you return your tithe, God will bless you and banish devourers. All manners of devourers were silenced in my life and family when I keyed into the principle of tithing. Wealth with devourers is frustrating. I pray for you that every kind of devourer in your life and family are hereby banished in the name of Jesus.

There are two kinds of wealth:

1. Wealth with sorrow

2. Wealth without sorrow

The reality of wealth without sorrow shows that there is a converse to it. Every coin must have two side-s head and tail. You cannot tell the story of God completely if you look at only one side of God.

One side of God says that he is love. The other side says He is a consuming fire. One side of Him says that

Jesus is the Lamb of God. The other side says He is the Lion of the tribe of Judah. One side of God says He is the Price of peace. The other side says He is the Lord of Hosts, mighty in battle.

You have to consider both sides. If the blessings of the Lord makes rich and adds no sorrow, what does the curse of God do? Whenever God curses a man trouble begins for the man. In 2 Kings 5:20-27, we see the story of Gehazi:

But Gehazi, the servant of Elisha the man of God, said, Behold, my master hath spared Naaman this Syrian, in not receiving at his hands that which he brought: but, as the LORD liveth, I will run after him, and take somewhat of him. So Gehazi followed after Naaman. And when Naaman saw him running after him, he lighted down from the chariot to meet him, and said, Is all well? And he said, All is well. My master hath sent me, saying, Behold, even now there be come to me from mount Ephraim two young men of the sons of the prophets: give them, I pray thee, a talent of silver, and two changes of garments.

And Naaman said, Be content, take two talents. And he urged him, and bound two talents of silver in two bags, with two changes of garments, and laid them upon two of his servants; and they bare them before him. And when he came to the tower, he took them from their hand, and bestowed them in the house: and he let the men go, and they departed. But he went in, and stood before his master. And Elisha said unto him, Whencecomest thou, Gehazi? And he said, Thy servant went no whither. And he said unto him, Went not mine heart with thee, when the man turned again from his chariot to meet thee? Is it a time to receive money, and to receive garments, and oliveyards, and vineyards, and sheep, and oxen, and menservants, and maidservants? The leprosy therefore of Naaman shall cleave unto thee, and unto thy seed for ever. And he went out from his presence a leper as white as snow.

As a son of the prophet, the wealth Gehazi received was enough to make him rich for a lifetime. But he got something extra for him and his generations – the leprosy of Naaman. This was because th e man of God, Elisha, pronounced a curse on him.

Mind the way you chase money. Be careful how you are seeking wealth. If you want money by all means, you will have it, but you will also have some sorrow with it. If you want wealth at all costs, you will get some serious trouble with it.

1 Timothy 6:10-11 says,

For the love of money is the root of all evil: which while some coveted after, they have erred from the faith, and pierced themselves through with many sorrows. But thou, O man of God, flee these things; and follow after righteousness, godliness, faith, love, patience, meekness.

Those who pursue money at all costs end up with sorrow of all kinds. If you want to be rich by stealing, inflating prices, by defrauding others, cyber theft, lying and false accusations, etc., you will get money. But you will get the curse of God along with it.

When we moved to the camp ground newly and we started building, some people exploited the church. I did not know there are different kinds and sizes of wood. I was not a builder, and had never built a house before then. They decided to exploit my ignorance. They made money, but when God moved, it was sad. One of them was travelling to Shagamu; the bus had an accident, and he was the only one that was badly injured. God did not allow him to die, so he could learn the lesson. The other person's wife was in a crowd; a car lost control, ran into the crowd, and hit her only. She was in the hospital until the man had spent all the money he stole from the church.

When we started building the current auditorium, one of my daughters came to me and told me she supplies granite. She offered us the exact price and promised to use her own trucks to deliver them. I was so grateful. She fulfilled her promise. Along the line, we did not know that the drivers were stealing some of the granites. They would load the truck, divert it somewhere else, and sell. They delivered less than what we bargained. One day, all the six trucks for delivery refused to start. They brought in the engineers and they serviced them. But they refused to start.

My daughter sensed that something was wrong and started querying the drivers. How could all six trucks break down at the same time? They even refused to start even when the engineers have done everything. She discovered that these drivers had been stealing God's granite. She found out how many trucks of granites were stolen. She came to the church and paid for all the granites they stole. When she got home, all six trucks started! I wonder what would have happened to those drivers. Many people, in an attempt to prove that they are wise become fools. In an attempt of trying to do a quick one, they pronounce a curse on themselves.

God is interested in the way you chase money. Therefore, be patient to prosper in a righteous way because the pains that come with acquiring wealth by unrighteousness is too great to bear.

Make a commitment to prosper Go'sd way and say the following prayers with all your heart.

Prayer Points

1. Father, I want to do your will. Give me grace in the name of Jesus.

2. Father, I do not want the kind of wealth that will bring me curses, in the name of Jesus.

3. Father, forgive me for stealing from you – in tithes, offerings, first fruits, etc. – in the name of Jesus.

4. Father, my life is open for your blessings, in the name of Jesus.

5. Father, whatever I have done in the past that has attracted your curse upon my life, forgive me, in the name of Jesus.

6. Father, grant me the grace to repent in the name of Jesus.

7. Father, let every curse that is existing in my life turn to blessings, in the name of Jesus.

8. Father, from now on I will do your will. Bless me so much so that others will come and ask me what the secret of my success is.

9. Father, make me a testimony of unlimited greatness, in the name of Jesus.

10. Father, remove every selfishness in me, in the name of Jesus.

11. Father, clothe me with the garment of patience to wait for your time, in the name of Jesus.

CHAPTER 16: OVERFLOWING GREATNESS

Furthermore David the king said unto all the congregation, Solomon my son, whom alone God hath chosen, is yet young and tender, and the work is great: for the palace is not for man, but for the LORD God. Now I have prepared with all my might for the house of my God the gold for things to be made of gold, and the silver for things of silver, and the brass for things of brass, the iron for things of iron, and wood for things of wood; onyx stones, and stones to be set, glistering stones, and of divers colours, and all manner of precious stones, and marble stones in abundance. Moreover, because I have set my affection to the house of my God, I have of mine own proper good, of gold and silver, which I have given to the house of my God, over and above all that I have prepared for the holy house, Even three thousand talents of gold, of the gold of Ophir, and seven thousand talents of refined silver, to overlay the walls of the houses withal: The gold for things of gold, and the silver for things of silver, and for all manner of work to be made by the hands of artificers. And who then is willing to consecrate his service this day unto the LORD? – 1 Chronicles 29:1-5

We have talked about the levels of prosperity in Chapter 11 of this Section. However, for clarity in this chapter, we will do a little revision.

Prosperity, as we have said before is in degrees. At the bottom of that category is destitution – those who eat their sons for survival. After that group, we talked about those who are poor. The Bible even says the poor will never end in our midst. It did not say you will be poor. The next category of prosperity we talked about is those who are comfortable. They merely survive from month to month. Their basic needs are comfortably met. Majority of Christians settle in this category. The next category is that of the rich. They have enough to eat and drink and have extra that they do not need in a hurry. But there is yet another category. Wealthy people have enough to eat and drink and save money that they do not need for a long time. There is still another level we call prosperous. There are not too many of them around because of the way they have been blessed.

I once went on a trip with an opulent man. When we went shopping, I was checking the prices of the items I picked up before I put in my basket. But I noticed that this man was just putting anything into the basket that appealed to him without checking the price tag. I asked him", Won't you bother to check the prices of those items?" He replied, "Oh! There is no need." He is capable of paying whatever is the cost of anything he wanted. Such will soon be your story, in the name of Jesus.

I also went on a trip to Dubai some time ago, and they pointed out a shop to me. I went there to shop. When

I got there, I saw a beautiful jacket, and I loved it. When I checked the price, it was

$10,000. What? I thought these people were joking. They also asked me to check for some shoes. A shoe there costs about $5,000. I shuddered; what? I asked them, "What kind of shop is this?" They replied, **"Oh, it is for those who don't check prices".** I pray for you that very soon you will shop in such places without feeling it, in the name of Jesus.

There is yet another level of prosperity called flourishing. These are the people who lend to nations. Nations call on such people to give them loans. I decree in the name above every other name that you will flourish. From the scriptures, the flourishing are described. In 2 Chronicles 1:6-12 Solomon offered a thousand burnt offerings to God in one day. In 2 Chronicles 7:5 he offered twenty two thousand cows and one hundred and twenty thousand sheep. This is overflowing prosperity.

In the key scripture in this chapter, David was also described as flourishing. He supplied all that would be needed to build the temple of God. He did not stop there; he also provided what will be used for the maintenance of the temple for several years to come.

There was a man who built a temple for one of our missions in the Eastern part of Nigeria. I have not had time for church dedications, but when I heard he was the one, I decided I would go. I am glad I did. When I saw what the man built, I scream"Tedh,e Lord is good!" He told me that he also built a house for the pastor behind the auditorium. In addition, he also bought two gigantic electric generators for the church. He did not stop there. He also put over six guards to protect and tend the church environment, and promised to keep paying their salaries for several years. As if that was not enough, he also bought an SUV (commonly called Jeep) for the resident pastor. Now, this is an evidence of flourishing.

Some of us want unlimited wealth, but what do we want to do with it when it comes? These testimonies I have told you were written down to teach us what these people did with the wealth God committed to them. God said this about David in Acts 13:22:

And when he had removed him, he raised up unto them David to be their king; to whom

also he gave testimony, and said, I have found David the son of Jesse, a man after mine own heart, which shall fulfil all my will.

I was praying about this text sometime ago and God said to me, "Son, tell my people; blessing them is no problem with me. I can make all of them billionaires in any currency. The problem is that I can't find a treasurer". God cannot find someone who if he gives the money, will use it for His glory.

The Almighty God is looking for a treasurer. Who will that treasurer be? The Lord is seriously looking. If you are the one, shout", I am the one!"

Prayer Points

1. Father, I know you are looking for a divine treasurer. Try me; prosper me, and I promise that I will not fail You, in the name of Jesus.

2. Father, make me a blessing to nations of the world, in the name of Jesus.

3. Father, I want to be in the category of those who lend to nations, in the name of Jesus.

4. Father, do not bless me alone; bless my family and neighbours too, in the name of Jesus.

5. Father, I will not hoard your blessings; make me a blessing, in the name of Jesus.

6. Father, beginning from now, do not let the sea of my finances ever dry, in the name of Jesus.

7. Oh Lord, let me always have much more than I can ever spend, in the name of Jesus.

By humility and the fear of the LORD are riches, and honour, and life. – Proverbs 22:4

CHAPTER 17: RIVERS OF LIVING WATERS

Poverty without any doubt is a killer. Proverbs 14:20 makes it abundantly clear that poverty can produce hatred.

The poor is hated even of his own neighbour: but the rich hath many friends. – Proverbs 14:20

In other words, a man can be hated for the simple fact that he is poor; no other offence other than that he is poor. This is why poverty must leave you and your family alone, in the name of Jesus.

As a matter of fact, in Proverbs 10:15 the Bible states clearly that the destruction of the poor is their poverty:

The rich man's wealth is his strong city: the destruction of the poor is their poverty.

In other words, poverty can cause destruction. The poor can be destroyed simply because of their poverty.

But since destruction is not your portion, poverty MUST have to get out of your life and family, in the name of Jesus.

Poverty Can Lead to Suicide

The Bible proves this understanding of poverty in 1 Kings 17:8-12:

And the word of the LORD came unto him, saying, Arise, get thee to Zarephath, which belongeth to Zidon, and dwell there: behold, I have commanded a widow woman there to sustain thee. So he arose and went to Zarephath. And when he came to the gate of the city, behold, the widow woman was there gathering of sticks: and he called to her, and said, Fetch me, I pray thee, a little water in a vessel, that I may drink. And as she was going to fetch it, he called to her, and said, Bring me, I pray thee, a morsel of bread in thine hand. And she said, As the LORD thy God liveth, I have not a cake, but an handful of meal in a barrel, and a little oil in a cruse: and, behold, I am gathering two sticks, that I may go in

and dress it for me and my son, that we may eat it, and die.

When you read this text with understanding, you will find out that poverty can lead to suicidal thoughts. The widow had just one meal left. Clearly, she wanted to prepare the last meal and commit suicide. If poverty reaches a certain level, it will cause people to say, "Death is better than shame."

Let me share this story. One of my uncles had it rough in his life. The level of poverty became so great that he decided to commit suicide. However, he wanted to do it in style. He decided to go to church, dance and worship so much that everyone will notice him. Then he would go home and kill himself. People would then say he was unknowingly celebrating his departure. Fortunately, when he went to church, the man of God was talking about Shedrach, Meshach, and Abednego. They did not know how God was going to get them out of the fire, but they had faith, and God delivered them. When he heard this word, it struck him. He said to himself; "I don't know how God will get me out of this kind of poverty, but I refuse to die!" As of the time he was sharing this testimony, he just bought 13 cars for his staff in one day! Your enemies may have thought that poverty will kill you, but they have failed, in the name of Jesus.

Poverty, therefore, can cause suicide. It can also cause cannibalism (the practice of eating the flesh of your own kind). 2 Kings 6:25-29 reports that when things were so tough in Samaria, two women living together held a horrible meeting to kill their sons to eat to save their lives.

And there was a great famine in Samaria: and, behold, they besieged it, until an ass's head was sold for fourscore pieces of silver, and the fourth part of a cab of dove's dung for five pieces of silver. And as the king of Israel was passing by upon the wall, there cried a woman unto him, saying, Help, my lord, O king. And he said, If the LORD do not help thee, whence shall I help thee? out of the barnfloor, or out of the winepress? And the king said unto her, What aileth thee? And she answered, This woman said unto me, Give thy son, that we may eat him to day, and we will eat my son tomorrow. So we boiled my son, and did eat him: and I said unto her on the next day, Give thy son, that we may eat him: and she hath hid her son. – 2 Kings 6:25-29

On reading this, you may think it cannot happen in our time. Some time ago in Nigeria, a woman was arrested for selling her son.

Everyone was pouring their wrath on her, but she insisted that we hear her story. She said,"At least, where the boy is going, he will find food to eat. I have nothing. From the money I made from selling him, I will survive for a while". This is the result of poverty. May a situation that will make you sell your relative never arise in your life, in the name of Jesus.

Truncation of Destiny

Poverty can cause the truncation (the act of cutting short) of a man's destiny. In 2 Kings 4:1, it is written that the widow of one of the sons of the prophet, reported to Elisha that her two sons were about to be sold by her husband's creditors.

Now there cried a certain woman of the wives of the sons of the prophets unto Elisha, saying, Thy servant my husband is dead; and thou knowest that thy servant did fear the LORD: and the creditor is come to take unto him my two sons to be bondmen. – 2 Kings 4:1

Her sons were about to be sold into slavery because of poverty. If they were sold, the possibility of ever becoming prophets would be very, very slim. The plan of God for your life will not be destroyed by poverty, in the name of Jesus.

On the other hand, wealth can be a river of life. Wealth can make life flow like a river. Proverbs 14:20, says that the rich has many friends. This is the opposite of enemies. There are a couple of things money can provide. Let us look at some of them one after another.

Riches Produces Dominion

Proverbs 22:7 tell us clearly that,

The rich ruleth over the poor, and the borrower is servant to the lender.

Riches can produce dominion. The rich will always rule over the poor. When God created you, His plan for you is that you multiply and have dominion. You are to be in control.

Money Produces Defense

Ecclesiastes 7:12 says,

For wisdom is a defence, and money is a defence: but the excellency of knowledge is, that wisdom giveth life to them that have it.

Money can produce security. Money is a defence. Money can defend you against attackers.

Money Preserves Destiny

Money can also preserve destinies. 2 Kings 4:-7, says it all:

Now there cried a certain woman of the wives of the sons of the prophets unto Elisha, saying, Thy servant my husband is dead; and thou knowest that thy servant did fear the LORD: and the creditor is come to take unto him my two sons to be bondmen. And Elisha said unto her, What shall I do for thee? tell me, what hast thou in the house? And she said, Thine handmaid hath not any thing in the house, save a pot of oil. Then he said, Go, borrow thee vessels abroad of all thy neighbours, even empty vessels; borrow not a few. And when thou art come in, thou shalt shut the door upon thee and upon thy sons, and shalt pour out into all those vessels, and thou shalt set aside that which is full. So she went from him, and shut the door upon her and upon her sons, who brought the vessels to her; and she poured out. And it came to pass, when the vessels were full, that she said unto her son, Bring me yet a vessel. And he said unto her, There is not a vessel more. And the oil stayed. Then she came and told the man of God. And he said, Go, sell the oil, and pay thy debt, and live thou and thy children of the rest.

When the situation of the widow changed through the intervention of God, she became rich. When the creditors came the next morning and demanded for her sons, I could see her laugh and say, "How much do I owe you again? Take your money and get out of here." She had enough money to live on for the rest of her life. I speak into your life: Receive the breakthrough that will take you far away from poverty, in the name of Jesus!

Fullness of Joy

Money can surely produce fullness of joy. In 2 Kings 4, the Bible talks about the great woman of Shunem. She was wealthy but had no son. It was her wealth that made her build a house for the prophet. This brought the prophet close to her family. She got a son as a result, and even when the son died, he was brought back to life by God through Prophet Elisha. If there is anything in your life that death has swallowed, it will vomit it now, in the name of Jesus.

This woman had wealth, but her joy was not full. But through her wealth, her joy became full. Some time ago I travelled to the USA for a program. When I got there, there was a car brought to carry me around. A lady bought the car specially to be used to convey me wherever I needed to go. When I left, she parked the car in her garage. Every morning and night, she would sit where I sat in the car and cry to the Lo"rdL:ord, I am getting old. Give me a husband!" After three months, she got married. Then she continued to speak to the Lord:"Lord, I am now married; I need childre"n.

The day I heard the testimony was the day she gave birth to a child in the hospital.

I pray for you: What will make your joy full, receive it, in the name of Jesus!

Your life is set up for greatness because the rivers of Living Water is about to flow into your life right now.

Seeking Wealth

As we have discussed, poverty is not an option. But the question is; how can we get wealth? Therefore, the how, when, and where you seek wealth is very important. If you seek wealth the wrong way, what is supposed to be a river of living water can become a river of killing water.

Jeremiah 17:11 says,

As the partridge sitteth on eggs, and hatcheth them not; so he that getteth riches, and not by right, shall leave them in the midst of his days, and at his end shall be a fool.

If you get wealth the wrong way, you will get it. But you will not be able to spend it. If you get it by stealing, falsifying records, defrauding, etc., you will leave it in the midst of your days. May the wealth that will kill you never see you, in the name of Jesus.

Joshua 7:16-26 records the story of Achan. He stole what belonged to God. This man secretly hid some gold. God brought him out and he was killed with his family. Be careful if you are stealing God's money. Do not die in the middle of your days.

Remember the story of Judas Iscariot in Mathew 27:3-8. He covenanted with those who were to arrest Jesus for twenty five pieces of silver. He made money but could not spend it. The same was the story of Gehazi. He received double portion of leprosy.

If you do not get money the right way, you will get sorrow with it. Job 20:4-15 says that the triumph of the wicked is short. Even though he swallowed riches, he will vomit it.

Knowest thou not this of old, since man was placed upon earth, That the triumphing of the wicked is short, and the joy of the hypocrite but for a moment? Though his excellency

mount up to the heavens, and his head reach unto the clouds; Yet he shall perish for ever like his own dung: they which have seen him shall say, Where is he? He shall fly away as a dream, and shall not be found: yea, he shall be chased away as a vision of the night. The eye also which saw him shall see him no more; neither shall his place any more behold him. His children shall seek to please the poor, and his hands shall restore their goods. His bones are full of the sin of his youth, which shall lie down with him in the dust. Though wickedness be sweet in his mouth, though he hide it under his tongue; Though he spare it, and forsake it not; but keep it still within his mouth: Yet his meat in his bowels is turned, it is the gall of asps within him. He hath swallowed down riches, and he shall vomit them up again: God shall cast them out of his belly. – Job 20:4-15

I have always told my pastors that if they steal God's money, it is like sandpaper. When you vomit it, it will come out with blood. When you steal what does not belong to you, the day you are shitting (the elimination of fecal waste through the anus) the money, it will come out with blood.

In 2 Chronicles 1:6-15, Solomon offered a thousand burnt offerings to the Lord. The Lord paid him a visit, and gave him a blank cheque: "Ask whatever you wan"t! Solomon demanded only for wisdom to rule. God decided to give Solomon what he asked and what he did not ask. In Solomon's reign, silver was like ordinary stone.

When God pronounced his blessings on Abraham, it reads:

Now the LORD had said unto Abram, Get thee out of thy country, and from thy kindred, and from thy father's house, unto a land that I will shew thee: And I will make of thee a great nation, and I will bless thee, and make thy name great; and thou shalt be a blessing: And I will bless them that bless thee, and curse him that curseth thee: and in thee shall all families of the earth be blessed. – Genesis 12:1-3

Abraham became very rich. Many people think they are rich, but you need to ask God to bless you. When you meet wealthy people, you will understand what it means to be wealthy.

Do You Want God To Prosper You?

Psalm 112:1-3 says, ***Praise ye the LORD. Blessed is the man that feareth the LORD, that delighteth greatly in his commandments. His seed shall be mighty upon earth: the generation of the upright shall be blessed. Wealth and riches shall be in his house: and his righteousness endureth for ever.***

Fear the Lord, depart from evil, and riches and honour will be in your house forever, in the name of Jesus. Be wise! Wisdom is the correct application of knowledge. Wisdom will teach you to copy what Solomon did and became the richest man in his time. The choice is yours.

Prayer Points

1. Father, I am tired of suffering. Open the door of exceeding financial breakthrough unto me, in the name of Jesus.

2. Father, open the heavens upon me, in the name of Jesus.

3. Father, that treasure house of yours that makes all your streets tiled with gold; open it unto me, in the name of Jesus.

4. Oh Lord, before this month is over, let me shout victory at last, in the name of Jesus.

5. Father, prosper me. I am tired of poverty. Prosper me, in the name of Jesus.

6. Father, I will use my wealth to further the cause of your kingdom. Prosper me speedily in the name of Jesus.

7. Father, give me an unlimited financial breakthrough in the name of Jesus.

CHAPTER 18: PEACE LIKE A RIVER

O that thou hadst hearkened to my commandments! Then had thy peace been as a river, and thy righteousness as the waves of the sea. – Isaiah 48:18

One of the most terrible storms that anyone can enter into is financial storm. All storms are ba–d things are not going well; things are turbulent. Storms signify trouble, fear, lack of rest, etc. Peace on the other hand signifies anything that is good, beautiful, and calm. Again, financial storm can be one of the worst storms that anyone can encounter. This is because financial storms can trigger other storms.

For instance, Proverbs 14:20 says,

The poor is hated even of his own neighbour: but the rich hath many friends.

In other words, if you get into financial storms, it can generate hatred for you from your neighbours. Your neighbours and friends can hate you because you are going through financial storms. As we saw in the previous chapter, poverty can make someone think of committing suicide.

In 1 Kings 17:8-16, with the widow of Zarephath, things were so hard with just one meal left. The whole city was going through financial storms. She decided to eat the last meal with the son and die.

Financial storms can lead to terrible things like cannibalism (women eating their sons as recorded in 2 Kings 6:25-29). Financial storms can lead to all forms of evil. I prophesy unto you: In the name that is above every other name, Jesus, financial storms will never come near you again!

It is financial storms that make people swallow charms, and consult the devil. If you know what some of the so called rich people do at night, it will frighten you. Some of them have to go to graveyards at particular times in the month to eat, in order to sustain their wealth. Thank God that His blessings makes rich and adds no sorrow.

On the other hand, financial peace can lead to other dimensions of peace. For example Proverbs 14:20 as we read earlier, also says that riches (financial peace) attracts many friends. In other words, the moment a poor person becomes rich; the moment the tide turns from poverty to prosperity, everything becomes friendship. Those who hated him before will suddenly become his friends.

Ecclesiastes 10:19 tells us that money answers all things:

A feast is made for laughter, and wine maketh merry: but money answereth all things.

Several queries in the past suddenly find answers in the presence of money. Money indeed answers all things. Ecclesiastes 7:11 sums it up:

For wisdom is a defence, and money is a defence: but the excellency of knowledge is, that wisdom giveth life to them that have it.

It is therefore clear that financial peace can lead to every other type of peace.

How to Achieve Financial Peace

It is evident that we all need financial peace. But the serious question is, **"How do we achieve financial peace?"** My prayer for you is that when it comes to financial peace, your peace will be like a river.

From the key text above in Isaiah 48:18, the Almighty God is telling us that if only we can hearken unto His commandments, our peace will be like a river. God expects us to not just read the Bible, but study it with mediation, in order to practice what it says. The Bible is the inspired word of God; it is not the voice of any man. It was not written to you by any pastor. Therefore, if you study the word of God carefully and obey, your peace will be like that of a river.

If you give yourself to the Word of God, you will discover that Proverbs 13:15 says that

Good understanding giveth favour: but the way of transgressors is hard.

Hardship is meant for sinners, not for the child of God. But if the child of God will not listen, he will be on the same level with the transgressor. In Deuteronomy 28:1-2, 11-12 state clearly:

And it shall come to pass, if thou shalt hearken diligently unto the voice of the LORD thy God, to observe and to do all his commandments which I command thee this day, that the LORD thy God will set thee on high above all nations of the earth: And all these blessings shall come on thee, and overtake thee, if thou shalt hearken unto the voice of the LORD thy God...And the LORD shall make thee plenteous in goods, in the fruit of thy body, and in the fruit of thy cattle, and in the fruit of thy ground, in the land which the LORD sware unto thy fathers to give thee. The LORD shall open unto thee his good treasure, the heaven to give the rain unto thy land in his season, and to bless all the work of thine hand: and thou shalt lend unto many nations, and thou shalt not borrow.

If you hearken diligently to the commands of God, you will experience financial peace on all sides. The blessings here are too heavy. You will lend to nations, and will never have to borrow.

Obedience in Details

When God commands us to do something, we must not obey in part. Part obedience is still disobedience. Our obedience must be in details. When God wants to prosper us he gives us instructions. In fact, God's instructions for prosperity are written all over the scriptures. But obedience to the details is what God requires. The summary of it is that whatever God asks you to do, just do it to the details.

In 2 Kings 4:1-7, Elisha commanded the widow of the son of the prophet to go home, shut the door, gather vessels, and keep pouring the oil. These were series of instructions for her to get out of poverty. The prophet told her what to do in details. Step by step, in detail.

Now there cried a certain woman of the wives of the sons of the prophets unto Elisha, saying, Thy servant my husband is dead; and thou knowest that thy servant did fear the LORD: and the creditor is come to take unto him my two sons to be bondmen. And Elisha said unto her, What shall I do for thee? tell me, what hast thou in the house? And she said, Thine handmaid hath not any thing in the house, save a pot of oil. Then he said, Go, borrow thee vessels abroad of all thy neighbours, even empty vessels; borrow not a few. And when thou art come in, thou shalt shut the door upon thee and upon thy sons, and shalt pour out into all those vessels, and thou shalt set aside that which is full. So she went from him, and shut the door upon her and upon her sons, who brought the vessels to her; and she poured out. And it came to pass, when the vessels were full, that she said unto her son, Bring me yet a vessel. And he said unto her, There is not a vessel more. And the oil stayed. Then she came and told the man of God. And he said, Go, sell the oil, and pay thy debt, and live thou and thy children of the rest. – 2 Kings 4:1-7

The widow obeyed the instructions to the details. Had she missed any of the instructions, no miracle would have happened. For instance, if she had gone home, got all the vessels, and kept the door open, the oil would not flow.

God expects us to pay attention to details of his commands if we must prosper. In 2 Corinthians 9:6-7, God commands:

But this I say, He which soweth sparingly shall reap also sparingly; and he which soweth bountifully shall reap also bountifully. Every man according as he purposeth in his heart, so let him give; not grudgingly, or of necessity: for God loveth a cheerful giver.

This scripture is a very popular one. But most Christians last paid attention to this verse of scripture the first time they heard it. Some others have never even paid attention to it. Many people even before they leave home to church have already decided on what they will give no matter whatever anyone says on the pulpit. Even if this verse of scripture is read over and over again, to most Christians it rings no bell. It is only a remnant of Christians that are grateful for God reminding them of this verse every time they hear it.

This verse of scripture did not just say we should give bountifully, but it also says we must do it cheerfully. To some, the worse time during service in church is offering time or calling for seeds. They keep wondering, "These people are at it again." That is why they are still having financial storms. But if you will hearken to God and change your ways, financial storms will end in your life today.

God is not poor. It is amazing how children of the Most High God have limited the Holy One of Israel. Again, God is not poor. I discovered a long time ago that each time I argue with the Lord over His commands, I suffer a lot.

In Malachi 3:8-11 says,

Will a man rob God? Yet ye have robbed me. But ye say, Wherein have we robbed thee? In tithes and offerings. Ye are cursed with a curse: for ye have robbed me, even this whole nation. Bring ye all the tithes into the storehouse, that there may be meat in mine house, and prove me now herewith, saith the LORD of hosts, if I will not open you the windows of heaven, and pour you out a blessing, that there shall not be room enough to receive it. And I will rebuke the devourer for your sakes, and he shall not destroy the

fruits of your ground; neither shall your vine cast her fruit before the time in the field, saith the LORD of hosts.

Here, the Lord explains why there are curses in the lives of many Christians; curses in their finances; why there are devo-urers because we rob him of tithes and offerings. Someone can say, *"Don't tell me that...I pay my tithe."* The question is, *"Do you pay ALL?"* Some pay some, and keep some. Paying in part is the same as not paying at all. Our obedience must be in detail. I learnt from experience that one cannot joke with God's commands. The problem with many Christians is that they do not learn.

As a mathematician, I used to argue with God over tithes. How can 90% be enough when 100% of my income is not even enough? What type of mathematics is that? By the time devourers were done with me, I learnt my lessons with time. Stop intellectualizing! Submit your brain to the Almighty God.

When I decided to start paying my tithe, God moved in ways I could not understand. He caused someone who owed me for five years to knock on my door at midnight and paid. I had forgotten about the money I lent him. He said he could not sleep. The money he gave me was the exact amount I needed to bind my research thesis, which I did not have. God caused my Head of Department to deliver my thesis to the external supervisor by hand. This was supposed to be posted. He also told the supervisor that he was not moving an inch until he read the thesis. Something that should have taken him six months to read took him just three days. What a mighty God we serve! All these happened because I stopped intellectualizing about my tithe.

I pray for you that whoever God has ordained to help you will not be able to sleep, in the mighty name of Jesus. God will surprise you. As you begin to obey God, financial peace will become your portion, in the name of Jesus.

Proverbs 3:9-10 instructs us to honour God with our first fruits. When you honour someone, you are giving something he does not really need. But the act of respect is what delights the person being honoured.

Honour the LORD with thy substance, and with the firstfruits of all thine increase: So

shall thy barns be filled with plenty, and thy presses shall burst out with new wine. – Proverbs 3:9-10

In the universities for instance, they give what is called honorary degrees to distinguished people in society. The degrees are given to people who really do not need them. They are not given to ordinary, peasant farmers or petty traders. They give it to eminent people. God does not need your money. There is nothing you want to give him that He does not have. But when you give him, you honour him. Besides, there is nothing you have that He did not give you. The hand you use to sign cheques was given to you by God. The brain you use in thinking was received from God. The fact that you have not lost your mind is because of the mercy of God. So, what is it you want to give God that He did not give to you?

Up till this moment you may have been just hearing. It is time to obey. I pray that God will quicken your understanding in Jesus' name.

Zechariah 1:17 says,

Cry yet, saying, Thus saith the LORD of hosts; My cities through prosperity shall yet be

spread abroad; and the LORD shall yet comfort Zion, and shall yet choose Jerusalem.

The prosperity that God wants to release is not for those who want to build a kingdom for themselves. It is for those who will build God's kingdom all over the earth. The Almighty God is looking for those who will partner with his kingdom anywhere in the world. I pray that you will be one of them. If you hearken to God's voice, your peace will be like a river. You will become an inexhaustible ocean of prosperity.

Prayer Points

1. Father, give me a hearing ear and an understanding heart, in the name of Jesus.

2. Father, give me the grace to do all your will, in the name of Jesus.

3. Father, give me the grace to do things exactly the way you want them, in the name of Jesus.

4. Father, beginning from now, financial peace like a river; let it be my portion, in the name of Jesus.

5. Father, let every financial storm in my life end now, in the name of Jesus.

CHAPTER 19: THE SECRETS OF OVERFLOW

And the word of the LORD came unto him, saying, Arise, get thee to Zarephath, which belongeth to Zidon, and dwell there: behold, I have commanded a widow woman there to sustain thee. So he arose and went to Zarephath. And when he came to the gate of the city, behold, the widow woman was there gathering of sticks: and he called to her, and said, Fetch me, I pray thee, a little water in a vessel, that I may drink. And as she was going to fetch it, he called to her, and said, Bring me, I pray thee, a morsel of bread in thine hand. And she said, As the LORD thy God liveth, I have not a cake, but an handful of meal in a barrel, and a little oil in a cruse: and, behold, I am gathering two sticks, that I may go in and dress it for me and my son, that we may eat it, and die. And Elijah said unto her, Fear not; go and do as thou hast said: but make me thereof a little cake first, and bring it unto me, and after make for thee and for thy son. For thus saith the LORD God of Israel, The barrel of meal shall not waste, neither shall the cruse of oil fail, until the day that the LORD sendeth rain upon the earth. And she went and did according to the saying of Elijah: and she, and he, and her house, did eat many days. And the barrel of meal wasted not, neither did the cruse of oil fail, according to the word of the LORD, which he spake by Elijah. – 1 Kings 7:8-16

May I begin this chapter by prophesying to you that from this moment onwards, you will never lack again, in the mighty name of Jesus. Beginning from now until you see Jesus in glory, your hand will never reach the bottom of your pocket. It does not matter what the situation may look like now; your financial overflow will start. The little you have will become big. The big will become bigger. The bigger will become extremely biggest. Your stream will become a river. The river will become a sea, and the sea will become an ocean. Before you leave this world, the world will talk about your prosperity, in the mighty name of Jesus. Shout hallelujah!

Every prophecy has a condition attached to it. When the Almighty God sets to do a new thing, there is always work ahead. This may include any form of spiritual exercise like fasting. In the story in the verse above, God tells us the secret of unlimited financial overflow; the secret of a never-ending blessing. The barrels never wasted. The cruse never dried. There must be a secret behind this unlimited blessing. This is what we popularly call in Nigeria",Sea-never-dry" (meaning, exhaustless wealth). In the mighty name of Jesus, that will become one of your names very soon.

It may be difficult for you to believe that your testimony will be that of 'sea-never-dry' because of your present condition. But you must understand that the mere fact that God has sustained you up to this moment should be enough proof to you that your sea will never dry.

Secrets of Overflowing Wealth

A. You Must Know the Source of The Overflow the widow here acknowledged the God of Elijah. She understood that there is a God who can change situations. Do you know God? I ask this with all humili"tDy: o you know the God of Adeboye"? If you truly know my God; that He is alive and able to do the impossible, your unlimited financial overflow is coming your way now as you read this book, in Jesus' name.

In Daniel 11:32 the Bible says,

"And such as do wickedly against the covenant shall he corrupt by flatteries: but the people that do know their God shall be strong, and do exploits."

Doing exploits means doing something beyond the ordinary. It only takes God to do something beyond the ordinary. To turn the headquarters of highway robbers to a beautiful Camp of the *Redeemed*

Christian Church of God only takes God. That God is still alive. It takes the God who can do the extraordinary to build our Church auditorium. When we drew the diagram for the building, we took it to America to source for steel. They did some rough calculations and told us that the amount of steel we need will cost about $66,000,000 (sixty six million dollars). I smiled. When we tried Egypt, they said it would cost $56, 000,000 (fifty six million dollars). We tried South Africa and they told us it would cost $52,000,000 (fifty two million dollars). Then someone said to us, "Why don't you try China?" So we tried China, and we bought all the steel we needed from there. I will not say the amount for some reasons, but the God who provided all the steel we needed for the church auditorium in our camp is still alive, and He is my God. Do you know him? Do you have a personal relationship with Him?

The widow admits that she knows the God of Elijah. More so, she knew that He is alive. One of the greatest statements in the Bible is credited to Job. He says in Job 19:25,

For I know that my redeemer liveth, and that he shall stand at the latter day upon the earth:

At what time did Job make this statement? It was at the toughest moments of his life. He had lost all his wealth and properties. He had also lost all his children. He had also lost his health. Job was at the very bottom of life – physical, material, marital, etc. But he did not care about what the situation seemed like. He only knew one thing: "My Redeemer lives!" Do you believe that your redeemer is alive? There is a God who can do the impossible. He will pay you a visit today, in the name of Jesus. All those who thought you are finished will come to borrow money from you, in the mighty name of Jesus. Know God. Let your faith be rooted in God.

B. You Must Love God– the widow knew she had only one meal left. But she was ready to do anything for the God she knew is alive because she loves Him. Do you know the secret of King Solomon – the richest and wisest man that lived?

The Bible records in 1 Kings 3:3;

And Solomon loved the LORD, walking in the statutes of David his father: only he sacrificed and burnt incense in high places.

Solomon loved the Lord. That was his secret. Also, in Proverbs 8:17, God wrote through Solomon to you and me";*I love them that love me; and those that seek me early shall find me."*

I have told people that if Jesus tarries and I die, I want this to be written on my tomb: "Here lies a son of God, who loved God. This is because love is more powerful than death. When you love, there is nothing you cannot do for love. I have seen love in action. God so loved the world that He sent his only son to die for our sins (John 3:16).

This widow was ready to sacrifice all she has because she loved God. It was love that made Solomon give God a thousand bullocks as offering. Like the widow, love makes you put God first in everything. I wish it could be said of Thee, man/woman loves the Lord."

When God asks for first fruits and other sacrificial seeds, it is a test. He wants to find out if you truly love Him above money. Do you know the thing about God? When you show him how much you love Him, He responds with how much He can love. No wonder He says that He loves those who love Him. God can overwhelm you with love. I gave God my first car, and since then, He keeps sending me cars after so many years. At one point I warned my congregation not to give me cars anymore. I do not need cars anymore. By the time I got home that very day, four cars were waiting for me. Two of those cars were from a Muslim. Just because I showed God love with just one car, He has not stopped overwhelming me with cars.

The widow gave her last meal, and God kept sending more and more meals. Everyone was dying of famine in the city, but the widow was looking more robust. I pleasantly gave to my God the very first house I built. I was not born with a house. So when God needs any house I have, I submit it because I love Him. Love God enough to put him first.

C. Trust God – when the prophet asked the widow to first make food for him before making for herself and her son, she could have responded, "Didn't you hear I said it was the very last meal? Where will I get the remainder for me and my son when I have first prepared your own. Elijah had told her, "Thus saith the Lord..." she just said, "Amen!" She simply trusted God. Although she could not understand how that will happen, but she trusted God blindly.

Numbers 23:19 says clearly;

God is not a man, that he should lie; neither the son of man, that he should repent: hath he said, and shall he not do it? or hath he spoken, and shall he not make it good?

When God speaks, it is done! Also in 2 Chronicles 20:20, God says;

...Believe in the LORD your God, so shall ye be established; believe his prophets, so shall ye prosper.

By God's special grace; not because I am more special than anyone; God has chosen to speak through me time and time again. When he speaks through me, He brings it to pass. He is saying to you now through me: "You will never be poor again, in the name of Jesus!"

You need to trust God. If you do not trust God, it does not make sense to pay your tithe. You will reason like me before that since 100% is not even enough, how can you make do with 90%? It took God to convince me, and my life changed forever. It is not scientific that you are still managing to survive on 100% and one pastor is asking you to give God a tenth of that. But the moment you trust God, the 90% will become too big for you to finish spending. He will start by silencing devourers in your life.

I do not know how God will prosper you. All I want you to do is to trust Him. When we were going to build the auditorium in our camp, God told me it would be between me and Him. I did not call for any offering in church concerning it. You need to come and see what God did if you have not visited our camp ground. Do you desire to know how it happened? - Ask God! A Bishop of another church came visiting and saw what we were doing. He sai"dY, ou are doing so much here". I replied, "It is God who is doing it". He then said, "Wait; I'm coming". He went into his car and brought a cheque of N25,000,000 (twenty five million naira). I never asked him for anything; he just gave. He came back after some time to share his testimony with me that in one year, God gave him $25,000,000 (twenty five million dollars)!

Here are the three secrets of an unlimited financial overflow: **Know Him; Love Him; Trust Him**. That is all. If you know God, love him, and trust him, you will be able to hand over the rest of your life to Him. If you put your life into God's hands, I can tell you with experience, that He is never going to drop it. He will not let a life put into His hands be snatched by Satan. If you put your life into God's hands, you will soon become an example to others. Therefore, I welcome you into an overflowing, unlimited, and unending financial abundance!

Prayer Points

1. Father, from now on, let my love for you begin to overflow, in the name of Jesus.

2. Father, you have all things; I am your child; let me have all things in abundance, in the mighty name of Jesus.

3. Father, because you overflow in health, let me overflow in health, in the name of Jesus.

4. Mighty Father, because you overflow in wealth, let me overflow in wealth, in the name of Jesus.

5. Father, because you overflow in power, let me overflow in power, in the name of Jesus.

6. Daddy, Your Word says that your streets are tiled with gold. I am your child; let me overflow in unlimited prosperity, in the name of Jesus.

7. Father, you have never been poor. I am your child; don't let me ever know poverty again, in the name of Jesus.

8. Father, you have never failed. I am your child; don't let me ever fail again, in the name of Jesus.

9. Father, I do not know how you will do it, but I trust you to prosper me, in the name of Jesus.

10. In the mighty name of Jesus, I say bye to failure," "Bye bye to poverty," "Bye bye to lack," in the name of Jesus.

CHAPTER 20: THE SUREST WAY TO PROSPERITY

The blessing of the LORD, it maketh rich, and he addeth no sorrow with it. – Proverbs 10:22

Supernatural prosperity is the kind of prosperity that will make you begin to lend to nations. It requires supernatural intervention. If God does not intervene, the devil will intervene. Those that go to wizards to use human beings for sacrifice seek some form of intervention beyond the ordinary. Although the repercussions are disastrous, they somehow understand that extraordinary riches cannot come by ordinarily going to the office and coming home every day. So they go and look for something supernatural that will help them transform their lives within monthsso they can become extremely wealthy. They are right in understanding that wealth comes from supernatural intervention, but their approach is wrong.

The type of prosperity we are talking about here is not getting a thousand here and there. It is the one that will get you to a stage where you do not have to think again before you spend. It will get you to a stage that you will realise that whatever amount you spend in a day will not even affect your capital. This type of wealth will frighten anyone who is not linked with the supernatural.

If you are linked to God, He will be the stabilizing factor in your life. You will not go astray. On the other hand, if you are linked with the devil and you get the type of wealth he gives, anytime you want to go berserk, the devil will remind you,"You have only three years more!" When people greet you, **"Happy New Year,"** he will say to you, **"Don't forget that a year is gone!"** This is a great limitation.

The key Scripture in this chapter says that only God's blessings come without sorrow. God has already blessed His children, but there are blessings, and there are blessings. There is what is called double blessings, compound blessings, or concentrated blessings. The question that comes to mind is", How do we get such higher levels of blessings? "

Greatness Comes Through Blessings

When a man who has authority to bless blesses you, the blessing is extremely powerful. He cannot even reverse the blessings, even if he has the authority to do so. If he is your father, husband, pastor, or spiritual father, if he says "God bless you"; he cannot turn around and say" I didn't say so". As soon as it goes out of his mouth, the work has started.

Genesis 27:33 contains a story you might be familiar with. Isaac had blessed Jacob mistakenly. But even when he found out, he could not reverse the blessings. In verse 33 of Genesis 27, he affirms that:

And Isaac trembled very exceedingly, and said, Who? Where is he that hath taken venison, and brought it me, and I have eaten of all before thou camest, and have blessed him? Yea, and he shall be blessed.

Jacob came, and by crooked means, got the blessings from his father. When the mistake was discovered, his father, Isaac, says, "I'm sorry. I have blessed him, and he shall be b"lesTsheed. blessing of a father is a very powerful thing. Someone asked me why I allow members of my congregation call m"e,Daddy." I do not really like it because it makes me feel old, but when they call me 'Daddy,' they are putting into operation a law they have learnt. When your father blesses you, believe me; honestly, you are blessed! Why? This is because a daddy's blessing is fully recognised by God, and He gives it His total backing.

How Does this Blessings Work?

Whenever a man is blessed, whatever he touches; whether a human being or material thing; blessings will be transferred to it. If you have any difficult child, do not curse the child. When you call the child and place your hand on him and say",You are blessed", you will begin to see positive changes. If you are a student and you have been studying one subject or another and failing, collect all the books on the subjects and lay your hands on them and say You are blessed!"

If you are a trader, as soon as you get to your shop, lay your hands on the door first and say, "You store, you are blessed"! If you are a government worker, get to work quickly tomorrow. As soon as you get there, lay your hands on the table where you work and say, "Table, as from now on, you are blessed"! if your vehicle has been giving you trouble, go there, lay your hand on it and say, vehicle, you are blessed!"

Many times, when I say things like this, people who lack understanding will say, "This man must be a big clown". However, before I make such statements, I have full backing from the Word of God. In Genesis 39:2-5, the Bible says,

And the LORD was with Joseph, and he was a prosperous man; and he was in the house of his master the Egyptian. And his master saw that the LORD was with him, and that the LORD made all that he did to prosper in his hand. And Joseph found grace in his sight, and he served him: and he made him overseer over his house, and all that he had he put into his hand. And it came to pass from the time that he had made him overseer in his house, and over all that he had, that the LORD blessed the Egyptian's house for Joseph's

sake; and the blessing of the LORD was upon all that he had in the house, and in the field.

The Egyptian man was a very wise man. He knew very well that whatever Joseph touched would be blessed. God began to prosper Potiphar, the Egyptian, because Joseph took control of his house. Honestly, when God blesses you, your colleagues will also be blessed. This is what blessing is about. However, there is a higher level of blessing; a greater blessing.

Positioning for the Greater Blessing

There is only one way by which you can get the greater blessing. It is by doing something special that will move God to bless you more than he intended. Talking about compound blessing, Genesis 22:15-18 says:

And the angel of the LORD called unto Abraham out of heaven the second time, And said, By myself have I sworn, saith the LORD, for because thou hast done this thing, and hast not withheld thy son, thine only son: That in blessing I will bless thee, and in multiplying I will multiply thy seed as the stars of the heaven, and as the sand which is

upon the sea shore; and thy seed shall possess the gate of his enemies; And in thy seed shall all the nations of the earth be blessed; because thou hast obeyed my voice.

God was saying to Abraham here that the type of blessing He would give him is an exceeding blessing. Abraham did something that moved God to His very Bein–g giving his only son. It took Abraham three days to trek from his house to the mountain where he had to offer the sacrifice of his son. This means that he certainly had a lot of time and opportunity in case he wanted to change his mind. Abraham remained steadfast. He even bound his son, lifted up the knife, and the knife was coming down before God stopped him.

Those who will get unlimited blessing from God will have to go beyond ordinary offering, tithes. Daily, you will look for an opportunity to do something special for God that will compel Him to do more than what He wanted to do for you. Those who trade with God never lose. Why you are where you are today is because God gave you a little, and the little is so precious in your sight that you cling unto it.

In 2 Samuel 6:14, the Bible says;

And David danced before the LORD with all his might; and David was girded with a linen ephod.

David was a king, but he danced so much so that everyone noticed and some mocked him, including his wife. This was special. God made David strong and wealthy. He operated in the dimension of the greater blessing. The rewards of David's dancing and doing special things for the Lord is found In 2 Samuel 7:8 when the Lord promised to establish him and his seed forever!

Now therefore so shalt thou say unto my servant David, Thus saith the LORD of hosts, I took thee from the sheepcote, from following the sheep, to be ruler over my people, over Israel: And I was with thee whithersoever thou wentest, and have cut off all thine enemies out of thy sight, and have made thee a great name, like unto the name of the great men that are in the earth. Moreover I will appoint a place for my people Israel, and will plant them, that they may dwell in a place of their own, and move no more; neither shall the children of wickedness afflict them anymore, as beforetime, And as since the time that I commanded judges to be over my people Israel, and have caused thee to rest from all thine enemies. Also the LORD telleth thee that he will make thee an house. And when thy days be fulfilled, and thou shalt sleep with thy fathers, I will set up thy seed after thee, which shall proceed out of thy bowels, and I will establish his kingdom. He shall build an house for my name, and I will stablish the throne of his kingdom forever. I will be his father, and he shall be my son. If he commit iniquity, I will chasten him with the rod of men, and with the stripes of the children of men: But my mercy shall not depart away from him, as I took it from Saul, whom I put away before thee. And thine house and thy kingdom shall be established for ever before thee: thy throne shall be established for ever. According to all these words, and according to all this vision, so did Nathan speak unto David. Then went king

David in, and sat before the LORD, and he said, Who am I, O Lord GOD? and what is my house, that thou hast brought me hitherto? And this was yet a small thing in thy sight, O Lord GOD; but thou hast spoken also of thy servant's house for a great while to come. And is this the manner of man, O Lord GOD? And what can David say more unto thee? for thou, Lord GOD, knowest thy servant. – 2 Samuel 7:8-20

If only you can serve God with all your strength all your life, He will turn around and say to you in blessing, I will bless you. In multiplying, I will multiply your you and your seed."

Prayer Points

1. Father, give me the grace to always desire to please you, in the name of Jesus.

2. Father, grant me the wealth that has no sorrow, in the name of Jesus.

3. Father, make me love you so much that I can sacrifice all I have for you, in the name of Jesus.

4. Father, may nothing be too big for me to lay down at your feet, in the name of Jesus.

5. Oh Lord, in the name that is above every other name [Jesus], make me operate in the dimension of the greater blessing.

6. Father, bless me indeed today, in the name of Jesus.

7. Father, let no power be able to reverse my blessings, in the name of Jesus.

CHAPTER 21: THE LAWS OF HARVEST

And there was a famine in the land, beside the first famine that was in the days of Abraham. And Isaac went unto Abimelech king of the Philistines unto Gerar. And the LORD appeared unto him, and said, Go not down into Egypt; dwell in the land which I shall tell thee of: Sojourn in this land, and I will be with thee, and will bless thee; for unto thee, and unto thy seed, I will give all these countries, and I will perform the oath which I sware unto Abraham thy father; And I will make thy seed to multiply as the stars of heaven, and will give unto thy seed all these countries; and in thy seed shall all the nations of the earth be blessed. – Genesis 29:1

Naturally, what you sow is what you will reap. There is no mix-up about it: Whatever you reap is exactly what you sowed. There are various factors that the yield of the seed depends on. One of the most important factors is time. The time of sowing is very important.

There is a time for sowing maize, and there is a time for sowing yam. This applies to every seed. If you sow at the wrong time, you will not get a good harvest. The question that naturally comes when you want to plant or sow is, "When is the best time?"

When is the Best Time to Sow?

There is a concept that the Bible teaches about sowing. It is the concept of sowing in the time of famine. The Bible says in the key text above that the best time to sow is in famine! Here, there was famine, which we now call recession, in the land. In the twelfth verse of Genesis 26, it says,

Then Isaac sowed in that land, and received in the same year an hundredfold: and the LORD blessed him.

Isaac got a hundred fold return as harvest when he sowed in famine. This does not sound scientific to say the least. As if that was not enough, look at verse thirteen and fourteen:

And the man waxed great, and went forward, and grew until he became very great: For he had possession of flocks, and possession of

herds, and great store of servants: and the Philistines envied him. – Genesis 26:13-14

Isaac became so wealthy that a whole nation envied him. He had a great store of servants, apart from stores for keeping food. This can happen to you also, if you learn how to sow in famine. Therefore, the best time to sow is defined by th*Leaw of Harvest*, which states that the best time to sow is in famine.

The Law of Unlimited Returns

The Law of Harvest, which states it is best to sow in famine, when combined with other laws of harvest, works better. The best explanation of this is that if you plant in a good soil, it will germinate and produce fruits. However, if you add fertilizer, the result will be better still. The Law of Harvest, when joined with other laws becomes the *Law of Unlimited Returns*.

For example, in Malachi 3:10-11, God says,

Bring ye all the tithes into the storehouse, that there may be meat in mine house, and prove me now herewith, saith the LORD of hosts, if I will not open you the windows of heaven, and pour you out a blessing, that

there shall not be room enough to receive it. And I will rebuke the devourer for your sakes, and he shall not destroy the fruits of your ground; neither shall your vine cast her fruit before the time in the field, saith the LORD of hosts.

God says, **"Bring all the tithes!"** Do not spend your tithes because God is not a beggar. When you bring it, you must bring it with humility, so that God will not reject you with your offering". Bring all the tithes into my storehouse", He says. He did not say", Help me spend it."

When you give God your tithe, hands off! This is when you then put a heavy responsibility on those who will spend the tithes. If they fool around with it, they will answer queries from the Ow–ner God. I can fight the whole world if I know that God is with me. But no one is able to fight God. When you give something to God and he asks some people to distribute it, and they do not do it as he asked them to, He will cane them. No one needs to explain to you that the cane of God is a terrible thing.

Let me tell this story about tithes. Sometimes ago, somebody gave me some tablets of soap. Normally, I give a tithe of everything I receive. So I gave tithes of soap. About a month later, everybody began to give me soaps. It came to a point where I had enough soap to open a supermarket. For a whole year, we did not buy soap. God never forgets. This Law of Unlimited Returns also removes curses from people.

The scripture above in Malachi 3:11 indicates that when you pay tithes, all the devourers that have been eating up your money will be silenced. This includes all the abortive efforts you have been making before.

The Law of Total Returns

The law of harvest can also be combined with the law of total returns. What does this law state? It states that if you give your all to God, God will give you His all. Prosperity does not mean wealth alone. There are some who are wealthy, but not healthy. Prosperity in the right sense of the word means you will also get to heaven. If you combine wealth, health, and ultimately heaven, then you have complete prosperity. How can you get total return, you may ask.

Mark 12:4-44 talks about a familiar story; the story of the widow's mite:

And Jesus sat over against the treasury, and beheld how the people cast money into the treasury: and many that were rich cast in much. And there came a certain poor widow, and she threw in two mites, which make a farthing. And he called unto him his disciples, and saith unto them, Verily I say unto you, That this poor widow hath cast more in, than all they which have cast into the treasury: For all they did cast in of their abundance; but she of her want did cast in all that she had, even all her living.

There was another woman, the widow of Zarephath, who also gave her all in 2 Kings 17:8-16. This was another widow during the season of famine. The man of God asked for water and she gave him. He asked for bread, and the woman said she had only the last meal for herself and her son. The man of God insisted, she sowed it, and she obeyed.

These two widows got total returns. They had some peculiarities.

- First, they sowed.

- Secondly, they sowed all.

- Thirdly, they sowed into the right so–il one gave to the house of God, and the other gave to the man of God.

- Fourthly, they sowed in the time of famine, when things were very hard for them.

- Fifthly, because they sowed all, they satisfied all the laws of harvest.

The Results?

- First, they had supply throughout their life. They never lacked again.

- Secondly, they became world examples. We are still reading and talking about them today.

The Law of Diligence

Finally, the law of harvest works with the law of diligence. The Bible says in Proverbs 22:29:

Seest thou a man diligent in his business? He shall stand before kings; he shall not stand before mean men.

If you want God to make you someone that will lend to nations, you have to be diligent in obedience. Deuteronomy 28:1 says;

And it shall come to pass, if thou shalt hearken diligently unto the voice of the LORD thy God, to observe and to do all his commandments which I command thee this day, that the LORD thy God will set thee on high above all nations of the earth.

God requires your diligent obedience in applying the laws of harvest. This will guarantee an unlimited prosperity for you and your generations.

Prayer Points

1. Father, give me the wisdom to know when to sow, in the name of Jesus.

2. Father, grant unto me the grace of diligent obedience to your laws of prosperity, in the name of Jesus.

3. Father, help me not to apply human wisdom, when I need to rely totally on you, in the name of Jesus.

4. Father, make me relevant in my generation, in the name of Jesus.

5. Father, because I will use wealth wisely, open the doors of unlimited prosperity unto me, in the name of Jesus.

CHAPTER 22: REJECTING RICHES

Many people are poor today because they refused to be rich. They rejected God's conditions on how to be wealthy. However, there are some that are poor because there are certain evil forces working against them.

There are several reasons why many refuse to be rich. Some fear that if they become rich, they will become targets of robbers and assassins. They fail to realise that if God gives you a car, He will take care of that car. If God builds a house for you, He will live in that building with you twenty-four hours a day throughout your life. You may say, "But I know Christians who lost their cars to armed robbers." That could be possible, but why should you think that the evil that befell Mr. 'A' must necessarily befall you?

Some people have their thinking caps worn on the wrong side, and they would always conclude that any evil that happened to anybody is also waiting for them. They are always hoping for evil, whereas the

Bible says, "Christ in you, the hope of glo"ry (Colossians 1:27). It did not read", Christ in you, the hope of deat"h.It is a choice therefore, to be prosperous or not. Choose to be prosperous.

God is good, and the Bible says that God is rich. There are several Biblical references to establish the fact of Go'sd unending wealth. We will look at three examples.

1. The Earth Belongs to God– Psalm 24:1 says tha,t " **The earth is the LORD'S, and the fullness thereof; the world, and they that dwell therein.**" If this is the only thing that is written in the Bible about God's status, it means that God must be very rich. Can you imagine a man who owns all the land of Nigeria, Africa, or the world? If you have travelled across the length of Lagos to Maiduguri on road, you will understand what it means to own the whole Nigeria. Moreover, if you have flown six hours from Lagos to London or fourteen hours from Lagos to New York, then you will understand what it means to own all the land in the world.

The Bible says that God owns all the land, and its fullness thereof. This entails all that is above the earth, on the earth (its surface), or in the bowels of the earth (under the earth).

2. Silver and Gold belongs to God– Haggai 2:8 says, **" The silver is mine, and the gold is mine, saith the LORD of hosts."** Anybody who makes such a claim cannot be poor. Silver and gold are just two metals in the bowels of the earth. There are lots of other metals and mineral deposits like coal, diamond, oil, and so on.

3. **The Earth is Full of God's Riches–** Psalm 104:24 says, "O LORD, how manifold are thy works! in wisdom hast thou made them all: the earth is full of thy riches." The earth is full of the riches of the Lord. No matter how rich all the human beings are put together, their riches cannot fill the whole earth. However, the wealth of the Lord alone fills the whole earth. God is not poor at all by any standard.

It is also clear that the closest friends of God were wealthy people. When Moses asked for God's name, the Almighty God introduced Himself **as I AM THAT I AM**(Exodus 3:14). He went further to say, **"I**

am the God of Abraham, the God of Isaac, and of Jacob." That means that if you ask for God's three closest friends, they are Abraham, Isaac, and Jacob. These three people that God calls His friends were by no means poor.

Genesis 13:2 tells us about Abraham:

And Abram was very rich in cattle, in silver, and in gold.

Genesis 26:12-14 talks about Isaac:

Then Isaac sowed in that land, and received in the same year an hundredfold: and the LORD blessed him. And the man waxed great, and went forward, and grew until he became very great: For he had possession of flocks, and possession of herds, and great store of servants: and the Philistines envied him.

Imagine a whole nation envying one perso–n Isaac. What about Jacob? Genesis 32:3-5 says,

And Jacob sent messengers before him to Esau his brother unto the land of Seir, the country of Edom. And he commanded them,

saying, Thus shall ye speak unto my lord Esau; Thy servant Jacob saith thus, I have sojourned with Laban, and stayed there until now: And I have oxen, and asses, flocks, and menservants, and women servants: and I have sent to tell my lord, that I may find grace in thy sight.

It is clear here that Jacob was not covered in rags nor was he hungry. God is also the God of the rich, and his closest friends are very wealthy. Therefore, if you become one of the closet friends of God, you become very rich. If it is evil to be rich, then it would have meant that God is evil. But God is not evil.

Birds of a feather flock together. The rich are friends of the rich and the poor are friends of the poor. When God befriends anyone, or anyone befriends God, they will become rich automatically. If it is evil to be rich, then God will not want you to be rich.

Beloved, I wish above all things that thou mayest prosper and be in health, even as thy soul prospereth. – 3 John 3

God wished above all else that these three things should be your portion:

- He wants you to prosper

- He wants you to be in good health

- He wants it to be well with your soul.

If you agree with God concerning everything else, how then can you turn around and say, "I don't need prosper"ity,or say, "Prosperity is evil?" If you cannot reject good health, why then will you reject prosperity?

Many look down on anyone who is well dressed. When they see anyone riding in a limousine, they will conclude that the fellow is not going to heaven. Who told you that? When I bought a certain car, some people started complaining that I had backslidden. They thought I could not drive the beautiful and long car, and make it to heaven. I told them I will get to heaven before them. The Bible mentions that God's first wish is that we have prosperity. Not prosperity with sickness, but prosperity with abundant good health.

Many Christians conclude that Jesus was poor, and so we must walk in His footsteps. That does not represent the Bible. The Bible says about Jesus in 2 Corinthians 8:9;

For ye know the grace of our Lord Jesus Christ, that, though he was rich, yet for your sakes he became poor, that ye through his poverty might be rich.

In heaven no one could be compared with Jesus in wealth. The floor of His Father's Kingdom is of the purest gold. He then put aside all that wealth and came into the world as a poor man. He did that so that He could be accepted by the poor and He might lift them out of the dust of poverty. He did not become poor so that we can be poor. Whatever Jesus suffered is so that we can have the opposite.

He died so that we may live. He was beaten so that we may be healed. By His stripes, we were healed (2 Peter 2:24). He descended into hell so that we may not go there. He thirsted so that we may not thirst. If you do not want the wealth that Jesus' poverty purchased for you, then you must reject His salvation that his death also purchased for you. You must also refuse the health that His stripes purchased for you.

Promises of Wealth

Isaiah 45:3 has this to say about God's promise of unfathomable wealth:

And I will give thee the treasures of darkness, and hidden riches of secret places, that thou mayest know that I, the LORD, which call thee by thy name, am the God of Israel.

What does God mean by the 'treasures of darkness' and 'hidden riches of secret places'? Until the discovery of crude oil, how many people knew the 'black gold' was hidden under the earth, where no one could see with naked eyes? What about diamond? Where do you get it from? What about gold and silver? The Almighty God is saying here that He will give you oil, diamond, gold, silver, and other mineral deposits as possession. You may have difficulty in believing this, but God owns all these things and can give it to whoever he wishes.

The reason why many are where they are today is because they are afraid to go higher. They simply pray, "God, just give me the money to rent one bedroom apartment". If you want to die poor, you will die poor. However, let me emphasize that poverty is evil. Do not let anybody deceive you that poverty is good. The Bible says in Proverbs 10:15 that

The rich man's wealth is his strong city: the destruction of the poor is their poverty.

Proverbs 14:20 says,

The poor is hated even of his own neighbour: but the rich hath many friends.

In addition, Proverbs 22:7 says,

The rich ruleth over the poor, and the borrower is servant to the lender.

If you decide to be poor, then you will be a slave throughout your life. This means that poverty brings hatred to you. You may not have offended anybody, but because you are poor, your neighbours will hate you.

James 4:2 says,

Ye lust, and have not: ye kill, and desire to have, and cannot obtain: ye fight and war, yet ye have not, because ye ask not.

This is the reason why many are poor: Instead of asking God to give you your benefits, you look at those riding big cars and feel they are not going to heaven. Who are you to determine who goes to heaven and will not? Rather than ask to be dressed like the lilies of the field, some prefer to wear rags.

Many people do not ask because they are not willing. In Isaiah 1:19- 20, the Bible says:

If ye be willing and obedient, ye shall eat the good of the land: But if ye refuse and rebel, ye shall be devoured with the sword: for the mouth of the LORD hath spoken it.

Some people think that the land referred to in the above text is in heaven. There is no land there. The land referred to here is on earth.

The Israelites rejected prosperity at one time. Numbers 29:5 says,

And wherefore have ye made us to come up out of Egypt, to bring us in unto this evil place? It is no place of seed, or of figs, or of vines, or of pomegranates; neither is there any water to drink.

God gave them an opportunity to have a land flowing with milk and honey. He asked them to go and take it, but they refused. Since they did not want the land flowing with milk and honey, God gave them a barren land; a land where they could neither farm nor find water to drink.

If you refuse wealth, do not blame God. If you remain poor, the choice is yours. God is good. His friends are rich. He has good thoughts towards you. He wants you to prosper. Poverty is a curse, and causes destruction. God wants you to choose one of the two– wealth or poverty. If you are willing and obedient, you will arrive at your destination and eat the good of the land. If you refuse, then do not blame God.

Prayer Points

1. Father, destroy everything in my mind hindering me from receiving your prosperity, in the name of Jesus.

2. Father, make me your close friend from today, in the name of Jesus.

3. Father, give me a revelation of my wealth, in the name of Jesus.

4. Father, banish any satanic bird that steals the revelation of your word from my heart, in the name of Jesus.

5. Father, help me not to struggle with your will of prosperity in my life, in the name of Jesus.

6. Father, give me my portion of the 'es arritches, in the name of Jesus.

7. Almighty Father, prosper me indeed, in the name of Jesus.

CHAPTER 23: THE WONDERS OF HIS NAME

And Jesus said unto them, I am the bread of life: he that cometh to me shall never hunger; and he that believeth on me shall never thirst.
– John 6:35

I prophesy unto you that throughout your life, you will never hunger. Throughout your life, you will never thirst. Whenever Jesus gives a name, He goes ahead to prove that He is what he says He is. Let me illustrate this with an example.

In John 11:25, Jesus says...

Jesus said unto her, I am the resurrection, and the life: he that believeth in me, though he were dead, yet shall he live:

Jesus called Himself the resurrection and life. Less than one hour later, a man who was dead and buried for four days came out of the grave completely whole again. This is because He proved His name – Resurrection and Life. At this particular moment, as you are reading this book, He is saying to you as it is written in the key text, **"I AM the Bread of Life "**:

From this moment onwards, your hunger will be over. Your poverty will end; not because the enemy wants it to end; not because the economists want it to end; not because your bankers want it to end (because they are hoping you keep borrowing from them and they keep making some interests); not even because the government wants it to end (when they are still struggling to pay N18, 000 minimum wage in Nigeria, then they are not in a hurry for you to get wealthy). But one thing is clear: Whether the devil and all these people want it to end or not, the Bread of Life will end your hunger, in the name of Jesus.

In John 6:5-13, a young man handed over his launch to Jesus, made up of five little loaves of bread and two little fish. He proved to everyone present that He is the Bread of Life.

When Jesus then lifted up his eyes, and saw a great company come unto him, he saith unto

Philip, Whence shall we buy bread, that these may eat? And this he said to prove him: for he himself knew what he would do. Philip answered him, Two hundred pennyworth of bread is not sufficient for them, that every one of them may take a little. One of his disciples, Andrew, Simon Peter's brother, saith unto him, There is a lad here, which hath five barley loaves, and two small fishes: but what are they among so many? And Jesus said, Make the men sit down. Now there was much grass in the place. So the men sat down, in number about five thousand. And Jesus took the loaves; and when he had given thanks, he distributed to the disciples, and the disciples to them that were set down; and likewise of the fishes as much as they would. When they were filled, he said unto his disciples, Gather up the fragments that remain, that nothing be lost. Therefore they gathered them together, and filled twelve baskets with the fragments of the five barley loaves, which remained over and above unto them that had eaten. – John 6:5-13

If you hand over bread to Jesus, He multiplies it. As Jesus broke the loaves of bread, people watched. But what they eventually saw, they could not believe. The more they looked, the less they saw. The bread that was multiplied was coming from the Bread of Life. The little you have in your hand right now, the Almighty God will multiply it, in the name of Jesus.

In Proverbs 11:24-25 Jesus says,

There is that scattereth, and yet increaseth; and there is that withholdeth more than is meet, but it tendeth to poverty. The liberal soul shall be made fat: and he that watereth shall be watered also himself.

This moment of your life, like never before, give more if you are tired of labouring; if you need favour. There is a world of difference between favour and labour. Jacob laboured for fourteen years to get the woman he loved. Isaac just went for a stroll and got his wife. One laboured while the other was favoured. You need to make up your mind to enjoy the favour of God from today. One of the things you will therefore do is to sow like you have never done before.

In 1 Kings 17, we learn that if you give God a cake, He will give you flour and oil on an unending basis, and expect you to do the baking. Do you know that God will open many doors for you? Are going to walk through them? God will not rain down money from heaven. In fact, there is no money there. But God can open mighty doors of blessings and expect you to walk through them.

Hebrews 11:6 says,

But without faith it is impossible to please him: for he that cometh to God must believe that he is, and that he is a rewarder of them that diligently seek him.

God rewards those who seek Him with open doors. He expects you to work through them diligently. Hard work is inevitable. This year, you will sing how great God is. In every facet of your life, God will prove himself. Before the end of this year, doors you did not know existed will begin to open to you, in the mighty name of Jesus.

Isaiah 55:10 says:

For as the rain cometh down, and the snow from heaven, and returneth not thither, but watereth the earth, and maketh it bring forth and bud, that it may give seed to the sower, and bread to the eater:

God will give you seeds and expect you to sow. There is food for eating, and there is seed for sowing. After you have sowed, God expects you to see that the seed is watered. Do not just give; get ready for hard work. Sowing is the easiest part of farming. One single fellow can start from one end to another, sowing in less than one hour. But when it comes to weeding, hard work begins. You have to get rid of the weeds competing for nutrients with the seed you have sown so that according to 1 Corinthians 3:6 you can say, "I have planted, Apollos watered; but God gave the increase". God gives the increase. Surely, God will increase you.

In the story of the boy I mentioned earlier in John 6, the boy did not just give bread to Jesus; he also gave fish. Jesus did not say He is the "Fish of Life," but the "Bread of Li fe". However, if you give Jesus more than bread, He will multiply it too. The boy gave bread and fish; Jesus multiplied bread and fish so much so that the boy went home with twelve baskets of bread and fish. When you give Jesus more than bread, He will give you in return, more than bread.

To illustrate this, I will like to use 2 Kings 4:8-17. The great woman of Shunem started by giving bread (food) to Elisha and later on decided to go beyond the bread to give Elisha an accommodation in her house. She did not need extra money in her life. She already had enough. In the name of Jesus, I decree to you that a day is coming when you will say, "I have enough money". God looked at her and knew that she needed something beyond money– a son. I pray for you that you will get what is beyond money, in the name of Jesus.

John 2:1-12, the Bible narrates a story of Jesus attending a wedding and the wine was finished. Mary approached Jesus to do something, but he appeared a bit reluctant. However, Mary told the people around Him to do whatever He asks them to do. Jesus then asked them to fill the jars of wine with water. The people there could have said to Him", It's not water they want; it is "wiBnue.t they remembered what His mother said. They filled the pots with water. Then Jesus told them to take the water to the Chairman of the ceremony. They could have sa"idS,ir, it is not water that the Chairman wants". But they remembered what Mary told them: "Whatever He asks you to do, do" Sito. they took the water, carrying it to the Chairman. How the water they were carrying became wine is something they could not understand. How God will make you laugh, you will never understand. You will not be able to fathom how God will give you unlimited prosperity. If only you obey Him to the letters, He has a surprise for you.

When you talk about signs and wonders, you can never beat the story in 2 Kings 4:1-7:

Now there cried a certain woman of the wives of the sons of the prophets unto Elisha, saying, Thy servant my husband is dead; and thou knowest that thy servant did fear the LORD: and the creditor is come to take unto him my two sons to be bondmen. And Elisha said unto her, What shall I do for thee? tell me, what hast thou in the house? And she said, Thine handmaid hath not any thing in

the house, save a pot of oil. Then he said, Go, borrow thee vessels abroad of all thy neighbours, even empty vessels; borrow not a few. And when thou art come in, thou shalt shut the door upon thee and upon thy sons, and shalt pour out into all those vessels, and thou shalt set aside that which is full. So she went from him, and shut the door upon her and upon her sons, who brought the vessels to her; and she poured out. And it came to pass, when the vessels were full, that she said unto her son, Bring me yet a vessel. And he said unto her, There is not a vessel more. And the oil stayed. Then she came and told the man of God. And he said, Go, sell the oil, and pay thy debt, and live thou and thy children of the rest.

The instructions given by Elisha looked like stupid instructions. The widow could have said,"I told you I need ed money, and you are asking me to borrow vessels. How does that relate to the problem?" "I told you I had just a little oil, and you ask me to still pour it out into an empty vessel?" "How will one bottle fill one vessel; let alone many vessels?" The secret to unlimited prosperity is this **B:lessed are those who do not argue with God's instructions**. This is one of my greatest secrets. I do not argue with God. He has asked me to do so many things that appeared foolish. I discovered a long time ago that my brain is too little to understand Him.

When God told me that the current location of our camp is our headquarters, I did not argue. It was far away from Lagos; the headquarters of armed robbers; without electricity; there was no water; the total number of cars in our church was about five. How were we supposed to move people down there from Lagos to this type of location? I did not argue with God. Today, you can see the results. If you will obey God in detail, He will perform signs and wonders. Imagine the amazement on the faces of the two sons of this widow as their mother began to pour out the oil in the bottle into the vessels. The oil never finished. It kept flowing until all the vessels were filled. They would have thought, "How could the oil in this little bottle in mummy's hand fill all the vessels with oil. talk about signs and wonders!

Jesus' Blank Cheque

In John 15:16, Jesus tells us He chose us; we did not choose Him:

Ye have not chosen me, but I have chosen you, and ordained you, that ye should go and bring forth fruit, and that your fruit should

remain: that whatsoever ye shall ask of the Father in my name, he may give it you.

Jesus has chosen us to win souls for Him and nurture them, and establish them in the Lord. It is then you can ask anything in Jesus' name, and you will receive it. Anything to ask for includes unlimited prosperity.

Finally, anytime you read Genesis 22:1-18, where God said to Abraham to sacrifice his only son, Isaac; something is striking. After Abraham obeyed God, God said, "…I swear…" Each time I read this text, I shake. If any of my children come to me and ask for a million naira, I will only promise to give him, and probably ask him to come back at a later date. He will go away very happy, knowing that daddy has promised to give him what he asked. I will not say, "I swear!"

God was so moved by what Abraham did (by giving Him his first fruit sacrifice) that he swore to bless and multiply him. Not only that, but that the whole world will be blessed through him. This is mega blessing. In Yoruba language, when someone has become so rich that it is impossible for his generations to become poor again, they say the person's wealth has become 'lame'. This means that the legs with which the wealth could have walked away with has been cut off. It will stay with the family through generations. In the name of Jesus, receive that wealth that will stay put in your family generations!

Make sure that from now on like never before, you serve God. Make sure that you give to God like never before. Also, make sure you obey God to the letters like never before. Put God first in all things. Win souls for God, and make sure they abide. I guarantee that so shall your exceeding financial breakthrough alight on you.

Prayer Points

1. Father, before the end of this year, that kind of blessing that I will say, "Lord this is too much", send unto me, in the name of Jesus.

2. Lord, I am tired of labouring; I need favour now, in the name of Jesus.

3. Father, showcase your signs and wonders in my finances, in the name of Jesus.

4. Father, give me a heart of winning souls for you, in the name of Jesus.

5. Father, give me the grace not to argue with your instructions, in the name of Jesus.

6. Father, take my brain; I submit it to your lordship, in the name of Jesus.

7. Father, let that which looks like an impossibility, become possible, in the name of Jesus.

8. Father, remove everything in my life that has been blocking my joy, in the name of Jesus.

9. Father, give me a pleasant surprise, in the name of Jesus.

10. Bread of Life, may I never go hungry again, in the name of Jesus.

CHAPTER 24: THE WONDERS OF HIS PRAISE

And Jehoshaphat bowed his head with his face to the ground: and all Judah and the inhabitants of Jerusalem fell before the LORD, worshipping the LORD. And the Levites, of the children of the Kohathites, and of the children of the Korhites, stood up to praise the LORD God of Israel with a loud voice on high. And they rose early in the morning, and went forth into the wilderness of Tekoa: and as they went forth, Jehoshaphat stood and said, Hear me, O Judah, and ye inhabitants of Jerusalem; Believe in the LORD your God, so shall ye be established; believe his prophets, so shall ye prosper. And when he had consulted with the people, he appointed singers unto the LORD, and that should praise the beauty of holiness, as they went out before the army, and to say, Praise the LORD; for his mercy endureth for ever. And when they began to sing and to praise, the LORD set ambushments against the children of Ammon, Moab, and mount Seir, which were come against Judah; and they were smitten. For the children of Ammon and Moab stood up against the inhabitants of mount Seir, utterly to slay and destroy them: and when they had made an end of the inhabitants of Seir, every one helped to destroy another. And when Judah came toward the watch tower in the wilderness, they looked unto the multitude, and, behold, they were dead bodies fallen to the earth, and none escaped. And when Jehoshaphat and his people came to take away the spoil of them, they found among them in abundance both riches with the dead bodies, and precious jewels, which they stripped off for themselves, more than they could carry away: and they were three days in gathering of the spoil, it was so much–. 2 Chronicles 20:18-25

Let me prophesy to you straightway: All the enemies of your destiny will destroy themselves in the name of Jesus. All those who have been working against your success, not one will escape; they will destroy one another. At long last, you shall be totally free, in the name of Jesus!

In the above text, we have a familiar story. There was a young king named Jehoshaphat, who loved the Lord. So the Lord thought about how he could make him very wealthy and found a way. He brought together three wealthy kings to attack his son, King Jehoshaphat. God made sure they would not go empty-handed. They thought they would run them over since the king is very young and his army is little in number compared to their combined strength. So they would go to battle carrying gold, silver, and all sorts of precious things. It was not meant to be a real fight. The battle would just be a run-over.

When these three kings were just a day journey away, news came to Jehoshaphat that three mighty kings were coming to attack him. He was very afraid. He did something very interesting. He ran into the House of God worshipping, and inquired from God what to do. The Lord asked him to calm down; after all it was not meant to be a real fight. He just wanted to make Jehoshaphat rich. All God asked him to do was to praise and worship Him; then he would see the wonders of his praise.

So, King Jehoshaphat gathered the choir with musicians, and they began worshipping the Lord. Somehow, the song turned two of the kings against each other for reasons only God can explain. When one overpowered the other, he also descended on the remaining king and they all killed themselves. No one was left alive. Then Jehoshaphat saw what God had plan–nead massive wealth transfer! It took them three days to gather the spoils of these three kingdoms. I prophesy to you: **One day when you take your money to the bank, they will close down for three days, in the name of Jesus!**

In Proverbs 13:22, the Almighty God says:

A good man leaveth an inheritance to his children's children: and the wealth of the sinner is laid up for the just.

For sure, the wealth of the sinner is laid up for the just. This means there will be tremendous wealth transfer. Do not let anybody tell you that Nigeria or Africa is poor. There is huge money in this nation. The problem is that the money is in the wrong hands.

Before the end of this year, you will get a huge chunk of it all, in the name of Jesus!

Qualification for Wealth Transfer

1. Worship

From the key text above, we discover that the number one qualification for God's wealth transfer is worship. When you praise God and worship Him, you will be amazed at what His response will be. Looking at the life of Abraham, you will discover something peculiar. In Genesis 12:7, the Bible says;

And the LORD appeared unto Abram, and said, Unto thy seed will I give this land: and there builded he an altar unto the LORD, who appeared unto him.

Genesis 13:3-4 also records:

And he went on his journeys from the south even to Bethel, unto the place where his tent had been at the beginning, between Bethel and Hai; Unto the place of the altar, which he had made there at the first: and there Abram called on the name of the LORD.

In addition, Genesis 13:18 says;

Then Abram removed his tent, and came and dwelt in the plain of Mamre, which is in Hebron, and built there an altar unto the LORD.

In all these Bible texts, you will discover that Abraham was always building an altar to God. People worship God at the altar. Abraham was an altar man; a worshipper. As a result, Abraham that left home almost empty-handed got the beginning of his wealth from Pharaoh (Genesis 12:16). **I pray for you that the one who God will use to** load you, He will bring you in contact with them, in the name of Jesus!

Jacob is another example. In Genesis 28:16-22, he had a dream, and God promised him some things. As soon as he woke up, the first thing he did was to build an altar for the Lord. He could not understand how he became rich as God had promised. By the time you read Genesis 30:27-43, you will discover that Jacob practically took over the wealth of Laban. Laban was a crook while Jacob was a worshiper. A worshiper moved in and cleaned out the crook.

Take King David for another example. He was a worshipper. He praised the Lord at all times, and God's praise was continually in his mouth. He danced with all his might. In 1 Samuel 27:5-12, you will see David raiding the Philistines and collecting their wealth. At his death, David was so rich. It was Solomon's wealth that did not allow us to know how wealthy David was. He provided everything needed for the building of the temple of God. He also provided for the maintenance of the temple for years to come. Some Bible Scholars say that the modern day value of what David provided for the temple is about four billion dollars ($4,000,000,000). David became rich by taking the riches of the enemies of God into his possession.

Isaac is another example. He was not just a worshipper; he made himself a sacrifice. In Genesis 22, he laid on the altar of God everything he was made of– his life! He never struggled with the father, Abraham. He willingly submitted to God to be killed. God then swore to bless Abraham, and multiply Isaac. When you move down to Genesis 26:12-14, there was famine in the land. The land was not producing food, but Isaac sowed. While other crops were withered,

Isaac's were nourished. The Lord transferred the riches of the soil of the Philistines to Isaac. He became so rich that the Philistines envied him because while they were bankrupt, he was prospering.

Until your prosperity makes a whole nation to envy you, you are yet to succeed. Until you are being criticised on newspapers, TVs, etc., you have not succeeded. Let them keep criticising while you keep succeeding. Trying to defend yourself will be a waste of precious time. Any quarrel that is motivated by envy cannot be easily solved. There is nothing you say that will make them happy. Great people do not envy small people. Only small people envy great people. You will continue to be head and not tail. You will be on top and not below. You will be first and not the last.

All that Jehoshaphat and his army did was to worship God. One of the wonders of worship is that it opens mighty doors of blessings. It brings in prosperity in a manner that you can never imagine. All you need to do is to look at what goes on around you and find a reason to worship God. When I was younger, I saw musicians become rich by praising people in parties.

They keep praising people one by one, until you are moved to spray money on them. Imagine what will happen to you when you praise the King of kings; the One who owns the heavens and the earth; the One to who all gold and silver belong to. Shout hallelujah!

For the next one hour, praise and worship God in your own way like you have never done before.

Praise Points

1. Father, put on me a garment of praise and worship, in the name of Jesus.

2. Father, there is no one like you.

3. Ancient of Days, I worship you. I bow before your majesty

4. Unchangeable changer, I honour you today.

5. I AM THAT I AM; The Lily of the Valley; be exalted forever and ever.

6. Miracle working Father, be thou magnified in my life for eternity.

7. Possessor of Heaven and earth; I surrender to your authority, and celebrate your sovereignty.

8. Father, I bow to your faithfulness and grace.

9. Oh Lord, receive my adoration and thanksgiving.

10. Rock of Ages I bless you for accepting my praise and worship, in the name of Jesus.

CHAPTER 25: SOUNDS FROM HEAVEN

And Jesus, when he was baptized, went up straightway out of the water: and, lo, the heavens were opened unto him, and he saw the Spirit of God descending like a dove, and lighting upon him: And lo a voice from heaven, saying, This is my beloved Son, in whom I am well pleased. – Matthew 3:16-17

In the history of mankind, nobody has influenced the world like the Lord Jesus Christ. Some may not like Him some may never accept Him as Lord and Saviour; you may call Him a teacher; you may call him a prophet; some may say He is not the son of God. Whatever you want to say about Jesus Christ, you cannot ignore Him. One thing is certain: whether you are a Christian, Muslim, or idol worshipper, you cannot ignore Jesus Christ. Why? Even dates that you write on paper has been influenced by His coming into the world. So you talk about years before Christ (BC), and years after Christ's death (AD). So if we talk about 2017, it means 2017 years after the death of Christ (i.e. 2017 AD).

Jesus is the most influential person in all of man's existence. Physically, the sick are still being healed in His name. There is no other person in the world in whose name people can be healed. In Jesus' name, captives are set free. Demons are still being cast out in His name. When it comes to material prosperity, there is no one who has ever lived who was more prosperous than Jesus Christ. No one on earth past or present can ever claim to have more houses than our Lord, Jesus Christ. Everywhere you go, you see houses built and dedicated to Jesus: Houses of the Lord. All these things happen about Jesus because He heard a sound from heaven saying, *"This is my beloved Son, in whom I am well pleased."*

Our elders say that if you want to be great, study great people. If you want to prosperous, study those who prospered. This is why when you want your son to learn a trade, you do not take him to someone who failed. You rather take him to someone who is doing the same line of business and has succeeded. If you want to succeed, study the successful. If you want to be influential, study the influential. If you want to be someone that the world will never forget, then study the One who the world cannot forget. If you want to be like the One whose influence is still on the world thousands of years after He had gone, study the Lord Jesus Christ!

A Little Study of Jesus

Jesus is the most influential, the richest, and the unforgettable. Before you die, may the world pay attention to you. Here are a few lessons about Jesus.

1. **Jesus was very Diligent**– If you study Jesus Christ, you will find out that He was a very hard working person. In John 9:4, He says,

"I must work the works of him that sent me, while it is day: the night cometh, when no man can work."

- Proverbs 22:29 says,

Seest thou a man diligent in his business? He shall stand before kings; he shall not stand before mean men.

Proverbs 21:25 says,

The desire of the slothful killeth him; for his hands refuse to labour.

It is one thing to desire be wealthy, influential and great. It is another thing to actually make it happen. Wealth, influence, and greatness are predicated on hard work and diligence. Some people want to sit at home and dream of success. It does not come from dreaming, but from hard work.

Jesus was Committed – He was committed to doing God's will. In John 4:34, Jesus says,

… My meat is to do the will of him that sent me, and to finish his work.

Jesus was a hundred percent committed to doing the will of God. He was so committed that He would rather do the work of God than to eat.

2. Jesus was committed to building the Father's Kingdom – not his own kingdom. Matthew 16:18, Jesus says,

And I say also unto thee, That thou art Peter, and upon this rock I will build my church; and the gates of hell shall not prevail against it.

God is looking for people who will build His kingdom. God is looking for those who will go and win souls. God is looking for genuine treasurers. A young man once said to God," Lord, keep all the glory and give me the gold. With the gold, I will build your kingdom so that You can have more glory". I think it is a very good prayer.

3. Jesus was Committed to Putting God First – in everything.

When Jesus taught the disciples how to pray, He first hallowed the name of God, followed by asking for G'sodKingdom. In John 14:28, Jesus says,

Ye have heard how I said unto you, I go away, and come again unto you. If ye loved me, ye would rejoice, because I said, I go unto the Father: for my Father is greater than I.

Jesus always puts God first. This is why the Bible says we should honour God with our first fruits in Proverbs 3:9-10.

4. Jesus Surrendered Absolutely to God's Will
– In Luke 22:42, He says;

Saying, ' Father, if thou be willing, remove this cup from me: nevertheless not my will, but thine, be done'.

In other words, Jesus always yielded His will to whatever the Father wants. Whatever God says must be final. I am not surprised that in Mark 12:41-44, Jesus remarked that the widow who gave all she had gave the greatest - total surrender. Yet some have a problem with tithe. Tithing just requires a tenth of what you have while we have a widow who gave a hundred percent.

5. Jesus Christ was Holy – In John 14:30 Jesus says this about Himself:

Hereafter I will not talk much with you: for the prince of this world cometh, and hath nothing in me.

Jesus refused to compromise. Today, there are many Christians who will compromise to get money. Jesus never did that. Also, money gotten through wrong will lead to sorrow (Jeremiah 17:11). Holiness is indispensible for a life of exceeding greatness.

6. **His Decision to Serve God was Voluntary–** John 10:17- 18 says,

Therefore doth my Father love me, because I lay down my life, that I might take it again. No man taketh it from me, but I lay it down of myself. I have power to lay it down, and I have power to take it again. This commandment have I received of my Father.

Your decision to serve God, to do is will, to surrender to Him absolutely, and to be committed to his Kingdom must be voluntary, if you desire a life of unlimited greatness. It must not be because somebody is watching. It must come from within your soul. Then the God who sees in the secret will reward you openly.

I believe that as you take these principles and begin to apply them, the Almighty God, who is watching from heaven, will call you out and say, "You are my beloved child in whom I am well pleased"! So shall it be for you, in the name Jesus.

Search your heart, and find out why with all your prayers and services you attend, your breakthrough has not yet come. Is it because God knows you are not diligent? Is it because God has checked your commitment and found you wanting? Is it because you are always ready to compromise if you get the opportunity? Do you need to witness more?

Search your heart at this hour and go to God in repentance in every area where you are falling short. Then ask Him for grace to live a life that is totally pleasing to Him. Such is a life of exceeding greatness.

Prayer Points

Father, I have searched my heart and I know that I have not measured up to your standard. I know that it is not your fault that my breakthrough has not come. The problem is with me. I am asking for your mercy.

BIBLIOGRAPHY

1. Adeboye, E. (2005). The Ultimate Financial Breakthrough. Ebute-Meta, Lagos: Printme Communications Company.

2. Adeboye, Enoch."The Wonders of Explo"its(Audio). Sermon, The Redeemed Christian Church of God, Mowe, Ogun State, 2013.

3. Adeboye, Enoch. "The Wonders of His Favou"r (Audio). Sermon, May Divine Encounter. The Redeemed Christian Church of God, Mowe, Ogun State, 2013.

4. Adeboye, Enoch."God Will Make You Lau"gh(Audio). Sermon, September Divine Encounter.The Redeemed Christian Church of God, Mowe, Ogun State, 2013.

5. Adeboye, Enoch. "The Instructor" (Audio). Sermon, April Divine Encounter. The Redeemed Christian Church of God, Mowe, Ogun State, 2013.

6. Adeboye, E. (2005). The Ultimate Financial Breakthrough. Ebute-Meta, Lagos: Printme Communications Company.

7. Adeboye, E. (2005). The Ultimate Financial Breakthrough. Ebute-Meta, Lagos: Printme Communications Company.

8. Adeboye, Enoch. "Great Expectation" (Audio). Sermon, April Divine Encounter. The Redeemed Christian Church of God, Mowe, Ogun State, 2014.

9. Adeboye, Enoch. "The Keys of David" (Audio). Sermon, April Divine Encounter. The Redeemed Christian Church of God, Mowe, Ogun State, 2014.

10. Adeboye, Enoch. "Secrets of Great Se"eds(Audio). Sermon, April Holy Ghost Service.The Redeemed Christian Church of God, Mowe, Ogun State, 2014.

11. Adeboye, Enoch. "Made Great by Grace" (Audio). Sermon, May Holy Ghost Service. The Redeemed Christian Church of God, Mowe, Ogun State, 2014.

12. Adeboye, E. (2013). From Austerity to Prosperity. Kilometre 46, Lagos-Ibadan Express Way, Redemption Camp: Printme Communications Company for CRM Bookshop.

13. Adeboye, E. (2013) From Austerity to Prosperity. Kilometre 46, Lagos-Ibadan Express Way, Redemption Camp: Printme Communications Company for CRM Bookshop.

14. Adeboye, Enoch. "Help is on The Wa"y (Audio). Sermon, June Holy Ghost Service.The Redeemed Christian Church of God, Mowe, Ogun State, 2014.

15. Adeboye, Enoch. "Help is on The Wa"y (Audio). Sermon, June Holy Ghost Service.The Redeemed Christian Church of God, Mowe, Ogun State, 2014.

16. Adeboye, Enoch. "Overflowing Greatne"ss (Audio). Sermon, October Holy Ghost Service.The Redeemed Christian Church of God, Mowe, Ogun State, 2014.

17. Adeboye, Enoch. "Rivers of Living Wa"ters(Audio). Sermon, March Holy Ghost

Service.The Redeemed Christian Church of God, Mowe, Ogun State, 2014.

18. Adeboye, Enoch. "Peace Like A Rive"r (Audio). Sermon, February Holy Ghost Service.The Redeemed Christian Church of God, Mowe, Ogun State, 2014.

19. Adeboye,Enoch. "The Secrets of O" verflow (Audio).Sermon, January Holy Ghost Service.The Redeemed Christian Church of God, Mowe, Ogun State, 2014.

20. Adeboye, E. (2013). From Austerity to Prosperity. Kilometre 46, Lagos-Ibadan Express Way, Redemption Camp: Printme Communications Company for CRM Bookshop.

21. Adeboye, E. (2013). Austerity Prosperity. Kilometre 46, Lagos- Ibadan Express Way, Redemption Camp: Printme Communications Company for CRM Bookshop.

22. Adeboye, E. (2013). Austerity Prosperity. Kilometre 46, Lagos- Ibadan Express Way, Redemption Camp: Printme Communications Company for CRM Bookshop.

23. Adeboye, Enoch. "The Wonders of His " Name (Audio).Sermon, January Divine Encounter Service.The Redeemed Christian Church of God, Mowe, Ogun State, 2013.

24. Adeboye, Enoch. "The Wonders of His " Praise (Audio).Sermon, June Divine Encounter Service.The Redeemed Christian Church of God, Mowe, Ogun State, 2013.

25. Adeboye, Enoch. "Sounds From Heaven" (Audio). Sermon, October Divine Encounter Service.The Redeemed Christian Church of God, Mowe, Ogun State, 2013.

ABOUT THE EDITOR

Taiwo Olukoyede (Nee Fakoyede) began his legal career in 1992 with the firm of *Chief Afe Babalola, SAN & CO*, shortly after being called to the Nigerian Bar.

In 1993, he joined *Chief Rotimi Williams' Chambers,* where he worked for several years before setting up the law firm of *Taiwo Fakoyede & Co*.

His published works include Contemporary Issues in Nigerian Law: Essays in honour of Judge Bola Ajibola SAN, KBE (1991), FRA Williams Through the Cases (2000), Current Law Digest (2000), and LandMark Cases in Nigerian Law: Melange for Hon. Justice M L

Uwais (2006) - all of which highlight major contributions to the growth and development of Nigerian laws and Legal System through CaseLaw and Law Reform.

Mr Olukoyede is a member, The Chartered Institute of Arbitrators, UK, and The British Institute of International and Comparative Law, London. He is the convener and co-director African Justice and Leadership Forum based in the UK.

Having completed the **_Bible College_** and the **_School of Disciples_** of the **_Redeemed Christian Church of God_** respectively, he was ordained a Minister in **_The Redeemed Christian Church of God_** in the year 2011. Earlier in 2010 following the leading of the Holy Spirit, he changed his surname from **Fakoyede** to **Olukoyede.**

Olukoyede has served in various capacities as Assistant Parish Pastor, Parish Pastor, and Provincial Legal Adviser respectively under RCCG, Lagos Province 29. He is currently the President, Elders Forum, **_RCCG Joseph's Palace_**, Dublin.

Taiwo Olukoyede is married to **Olufemi,** a minister in *RCCG*, and they are blessed with four children, all of whom are dedicated church workers.

Made in the USA
Columbia, SC
06 March 2024

32741356R00195